Climbing

Mountains

Jean Ellen Sullenberger

Dedication

As I think, not only of my journey but of the process of this book, I would be remiss if I did not take time to thank several people.

1. Jesus, without whom I would truly be nothing. In fact, I literally would not even be here to write this book. The miracles He has done in my life are overwhelming and often leave me speechless. Thankful is an understatement.

2. Pastor William and Jane Pellum who have loved and supported me for years – even in some of the most difficult times in which my hurt pushed them away.

Pastor's encouragement, which manifest in several different ways, when God told me to write this book was a confirmation, a push, and a constant reminder that if we know what to do and we do not do it to us that is sin. (James 4:17)

3. My brother, Daniel, for his continual encouragement and suggestions.

4. Dolly Kroeger for loving me and being patient with me in a time of my life when I felt and believed I was very unlovable.

5. The group of my students' parents who interceded for me and did an intervention at a time when I was truly falling apart.

6. Sandy – my amazing, patient, strong, persistent, and relentless counselor.

I strive to counsel after the model you provided.

7. Polly Anderson, my dear friend who prayed and believed that she would be with me when that landmark moment of healing and deliverance took place. She was.

8. Sheri Miller, one of the very first people I told my story to. Her love, friendship, encouragement, and support through many ups and downs, twists and turns, long nights, laughter and tears are second to none.

9. Sharon Metzger, my friend and my editor. She has encouraged, challenged, held me accountable, pushed, done things with my book I could never do and loved me deeply. I am extremely grateful for her and her many talents. Truly none of this would be possible without her. I write it, she makes it come together. God put an amazing team together.

Contents

Introduction

In Deuteronomy chapter 4, Moses is providing instruction to the Israelites and in the midst of that instruction he reminds them or reviews with them what God has done for them over the years. As he reviews, I can almost picture a crowd completely silent as they soak it all in. Perhaps some of them were remembering all the time they spent complaining or doubting because, after all, in the midst of the trial the road seems dark and we tend to focus on what is in front of us instead of what we know God can do. Others are shaking their heads in agreement as Moses delivers the address; no doubt Caleb and Joshua are in that group. I am sure Caleb and Joshua had some rough days on the journey but they remained faithful through it all, not forgetting what God had done. Perhaps some are smiling, some are contemplating, some are crying, some are peaceful, some are processing lightly and some deeply. No matter what group, all were taking a walk down memory lane and hearing again all the times God had provided. He provided food, shelter, protection, guidance, discipline, and many other things over and over again. After a little bit of review, Moses says in verse 9 "Only be careful, and watch yourselves closely so that you do not forget the things your eyes have seen or let them slip from your heart as long as you live. Teach them to your children and to their children after them." Moses is instructing them to testify. Pass along what God has done for them. What He brought them out of, the provisions on the journey, and then finally as they enter the Promised Land to never forget how they got there. "Do not forget the things your eyes have seen!" In verse 35, Moses says "you were shown these things so that you might know that the Lord is God; besides Him there is no other." Pass it on. Tell it. Make sure future generations know that the Lord your God brought you out.

We all have deserts in life. Times when we don't know where we are or what we are doing and the darkness becomes overwhelming; we are not completely sure how we got where we are and we certainly don't know how to get out. We've prayed, we've tried various things, we've believed but we are just stuck. It seems like the miraculous is for everyone else. We trudge along wishing that our joy would come in the morning but never believing it is really for us. It's been too long. God doesn't see me. Where was He when that was happening? On one hand, we read the story of the Israelites' journey and are frustrated with them for, what seems like to us, so easily forgetting the provisions of the Lord. On the other hand, if we were honest; how often are we much like the Israelites? Maybe you are reading this and have zero idea what I am referring to when writing about the Israelites. Whether or not you know the story, perhaps you are mad at God because the life you have lived was anything but fair. You long to be free from the pain, free from the questions, free from the confusion, but have little hope that it will ever happen.

The book you are holding in your hands is the true story of one person. Unfair life, yes. Pain, disappointments, and heartache, yes. Breath taking grief, loss of identity, confusion, hurt, betrayal, and trust stripped away, yes. Desiring to have a close relationship with God Almighty but never believing His love was for her, yes. Emptiness, loneliness, depression, suicidal thoughts and actions, yes. Turning to other things to fill the void, yes. Running from the pain, yes. Hitting complete rock bottom, yes. Climbing out, finding hope, working hard on herself, allowing God to be God and currently living a joy-filled, productive, peaceful life......YES!

Moses instructs us to pass on our stories, as I pass on mine to you my hope is that in these pages you too will begin to find hope. That you will begin to realize that you are loved, you are valuable and you do have a wonderful purpose. You do not have to be stuck in the pain of your past or present. Grab a cup of coffee and let's journey together.

1. <u>Bicycles, Straw Piles & the Red Plaid Jumper</u>

Sometime around age 6 or 7, I remember putting on my favorite jumper to go to school. I wore it with a white blouse. It was a red plaid jumper with black velvet straps and gold buttons. It was not only my favorite jumper but it was, by far, my favorite outfit. The day at school must have been typical but what awaited me when I arrived home was anything but typical. I will never know why there were four guys waiting for me to do sexual acts that no baby should have to experience. I do not know why those same four guys eventually grew their group to 12 and for the next 6 years of my life I was having some type of sexual contact with individuals or groups at the minimum of three times a week.

I had a friend that lived not far down the street. I would often ride my bike to her house to play for a while after school. We lived on a major highway so I would cross at the light then take alleys to get safely to my home. One day as I rode my bike past our barn one of the oldest guys was waiting at the corner. He pulled me off my bike and into the barn where he laid me on the piles of straw to fulfill his desires. My understanding of love was warped quickly as each time he did this he would whisper in my ear over and over, "I love you". This continued for quite sometime. I'd try to ride really fast past the barn or attempt to cut through my yard but he knew our property well and so each attempt was met with ridicule and him overpowering the little girl on the bike. I finally stopped going to my friend's house as often because I just didn't want to ride my bike down the alley. Many times on these days after brushing the straw off of my clothing and out of my hair, I would walk into my house only to get in trouble for being late. Please keep in mind that on those days, my mother had no idea what had just taken place and why I was late getting home so her scolding for being late was an appropriate response from a parent who had been disobeyed. Of course, unknown to anyone but me, in my little mind it was just insult on top of injury. How could I be so visible and so invisible all at the same time? Brokenness became my friend and silence was my escape. I withdrew and became very quiet. It was played off as shyness but the truth was, I was scared of everything and everybody. I talked occasionally but mostly to close family members. I distinctly remember one evening after a parent-teacher conference my mother saying to me, "Sweetie, you have got to talk, your teachers think you can't."

The abuse continued. The barn became a place of torture for me. Not only was I being pulled off my bike and into the back of the barn where the straw piles were by the individual but I was also being abused by the group in the upstairs of the barn. My father had created a weightlifting area, equipped with varying sizes of weights, and of course the weight bench. He allowed others to use this area as long as they followed his number one rule; none of us could be up there without a "spotter" because lifting weights by yourself is dangerous. I was climbing up the ladder to be a "spotter", why a little girl was an approved spotter I will never know but nevertheless I was, as I reached the top of the ladder to step into the upstairs of the barn I saw them all gathered around the weight bench. At that point it was too late to escape and just as I feared upon seeing them, I was laid on the bench and they began taking turns. Over the years I was told what would be done, I was occasionally shown pictures of what they wanted to do. I listened to them argue when one would take a little longer than his allotted time. The times I decided to fight back I was laughed at and the oldest person in the group convinced the others that they would have to hold me down while everyone took their turns. My arms would be lifted above my head and held so I could not fight. As the years progressed the group varied in size and eventually

13

dissipated. Some moved away, others just stopped. The individuals continued until finally my sixth-grade year arrived. My monthly cycle began and the abuse stopped. As a result of the abuse and a hostile home environment, over the years I became a people pleaser with an extremely low view of self. I put a lock on my heart and thus began to build a wall. The abuse had stripped my identity and left me lost in a sea of pain.

The question most often posed by survivors of any type of trauma or abuse is where was God? Why didn't He stop them or it? If God really loved me this wouldn't have happened! When we are hurting, we tend to immediately blame whatever is causing the hurt on God; after all He's all powerful, He could stop it. Take a journey with me in Genesis chapters two and three.

Genesis chapter 2 provides us with a more detailed explanation of the sixth day of creation. It beautifully describes the Garden of Eden and all the rivers that flow in and out. It says that God placed the man He had created in the garden. In verse 16 and 17 we read the command given to Adam. "And the Lord God commanded the man, "You are free to eat from any tree in the garden; but you must not eat from the tree of the knowledge of good and evil, for when you eat of it you will surely die." Verses 18-25 describe the thought process and creation of Eve. Here they are in this beautiful garden with rivers, trees, animals, and plenty to eat. It is not written out for us, but I think it is safe to assume that just as God had instructed Adam about the trees, Adam had instructed Eve. Beginning of chapter 3 we read about the introduction of the serpent. If Eve had no knowledge of what God commanded, the serpent could not have had the conversation with her that he did. "Now the serpent was more crafty than any of the wild animals the Lord God had made. He said to the woman, "Did God *really* say, 'you must not eat from any tree in the garden'?" The first place the enemy goes is your mind and that is exactly what he did here. If someone or something can control your mind they can control you, which is why the enemy always attacks our minds first. He cleverly got into Eve's mind and twisted what God had said. As a result, her response to him added details that God did not say and the deception was begun. In this case, the enemy was successful in sneaking in and getting them to focus on the one thing they didn't have instead of everything they did. The enemy trapped them and then they made a choice. They chose to eat. They chose. In that moment their conscious was opened, the Bible says their eyes were opened. In that moment the innocence that God so beautifully set into motion was destroyed. They did not physically die, they spiritually died. Make sure you get this;

the innocence was destroyed by a human choice, not by a loving God. My innocence was destroyed by a human choice, not by a loving God. The enemy does not come to discuss, he comes to destroy. I like this explanation Beth Moore provides in her book *Get Out of That Pit,* "satan has no more effective weapon in his arsenal than to make us question – not so much whether God exists, but whether God is really good. He knows God alone possesses the power and passion for us to be restored after nearly being shredded in life's killing fields. For satan to talk us into distrusting God and distancing ourselves from Him is to keep us broken, ineffective and frankly out of his hair." (p. 39)

2. <u>Rabbit Cages & Dollar Signs</u>

Every summer brought the excitement of spending an entire week at each Grandparents' house and sometimes other family members' homes as well. Before I was born my dad had accepted a job about 80 miles from the rest of his and Mom's family so although within driving distance Grandparents were not just right down the street. Weekend visits throughout the year happened but summer was the exciting time. It was a time to breathe, relax, have fun, and be a kid. We occasionally would go with another sibling but more often than not our time at Grandma's and Grandpa's was our week. Snapping beans, working in the garden, running around the farm, going to quilting Tuesday's with Grandma, playing with cousins, riding bikes, swimming, lemonade stands, and Root beer floats. The most exciting day for me, as a kid at both Grandparents' was Friday. Friday was shopping day, and at one set that always included a trip to Friendly's restaurant for dinner and ice cream. Grandma and I used to get the largest sundae, which when I was little was huge! Usually we would get Reese's Pieces and we would laugh when they set it on the table. Even together we couldn't finish it.

Both Grandmas made sure we came with play clothes and Sunday clothes. When you were at Grandma's house you went to church. One Grandma loved to play the piano and sing hymns. She did not do it as often as I would have liked but when she headed to the piano I'd get so excited. She could make those keys sing and she would get the biggest smile on her face as she played and sang. Sometimes after a singing session she'd just walk around the house clapping, humming or singing, and smiling. The only thing I was afraid of at Grandmas was the chickens. When she'd say it was time to gather eggs, my excitement bubble busted. I did not like going into the chicken coop. It was a good size building for chickens and they just ran everywhere; not my cup of tea. If we forget the chickens, both houses were safe and fun.

When I was about eight or nine years old, I went to spend my week with one set of Grandparents, who at the time were trying to help someone out and so an older girl was staying with them. The usual was when Grandpa left for work in the afternoon, he would take me with him, drop me off at Grandma's work and I'd hang out in the cafeteria until Grandma got off of work. They always gave me money for a snack and she would check on me every few minutes. I usually took a coloring book or some other little thing to keep me occupied until her shift was over and we would head for home. That summer everything changed. The other girl was old enough to babysit and there was a family down the street that had agreed to be the go-to for an emergency. They thought it would be fun for me to have more play time and not have to go sit at a job site, and it should have been. Of course, it didn't happen suddenly; it was over the course of a few stays. It started with comments and progressed to inappropriate touching. She would force me to do things I didn't want to do but her personality and size were no match for my shyness and smallness. It progressed to her dressing me up, putting make up on me, doing my hair, taking pictures, and setting up visitors. She timed it perfectly and was in complete control. She knew exactly when to stop everything, wash the makeup off and have me put my play clothes back on so all looked normal when Grandma arrived home from work. Although all of it was horrifying, I distinctly remember one day she did my hair, put make up on, put me in a little sailor's outfit and told me to follow her outside for a surprise. Near the garage, positioned so you really could hide between them and the garage, Grandpa had a set of rabbit cages. We walked to them and much to my dismay there were two boys waiting there. She looked at them and said, "Here she is have fun", turned, and walked back out. One was about her age and the other was in his twenties. A few years later when he apologized to me, he told me at the time he was 23. Thankfully it was nothing compared to what I was used to. A lot of inappropriate touching and kissing but nothing beyond that. By that point, I had pretty well learned how to not be present when things were happening to me. In the psychology field, we call it disassociation and I was a pro. It felt like an eternity, so I truly have no idea how long it was but I remember her coming back and telling them their time was up, taking me back inside, and getting me all cleaned up for Grandma's arrival. Friday finally came and the usual pattern of leaving with Grandpa returned because it was shopping day. I was never so happy for a Friday. At one of the stores, the bombshell and realization hit as the girl picked up something she wanted to buy. Grandma told her to put it back and she said, "But I have my own money". When asked where she got it, she explained that she had saved it at different points and just thought she would bring it with her today. Then as soon as she was able, she pulled me aside and told me in a very stern voice that if I said one word about where she got the money, I would be very sorry. I realized then, that although I didn't see the exchange, she had made the money off of me. She earned more money over the next few visits. Rabbit cages and dollar signs. One more lock on my heart, one more brick in the wall.

I found out several years later when I confronted her about these things, that she only did it to me because she had been hurt by someone and she just wanted someone else to feel the hurt she had. Little did she know how well I already knew the pain. She was the exact opposite of me. She was loud; controlling, could be very mean and just wanted others to suffer like she had. I, on the other hand overall, was quiet, gentle and never ever wanted anyone to experience the hurt I had experienced. We had very different personalities but I would venture to say our view of self was pretty similar. Worthless, unlovable, tainted.

In Numbers chapter 13, we read about the exploration of Canaan, the land the Lord is giving to the Israelites. God commands Moses to send some men to check it out. Moses does just that and provides specifics on what they are to look for. The men head out to do their exploring and collecting and return after forty days. They came back and reported to Moses, Aaron, and the whole Israelite community all they had seen and presented the fruit they had collected. You can almost hear the excitement in their voices as they declare that the land did flow with milk and honey just as the Lord had said it would, however, in verse 28 they take their eyes off of the promise and allow fear to set in. One word; "but". There is an exchange between them and Caleb as Caleb tries to remind them that the land is already theirs because the Lord promised it. The people refused to hear Caleb's words and said "We can't attack those people; they are stronger than we are." And they spread among the Israelites a bad report about the land they had explored. They said, "The land we explored devours those living in it. All the people we saw there are of great size. We saw the Nephilim there (the descendants of Anak come from the Nephilim). We seemed like grasshoppers *in our own eyes*, and we looked the same to them." Verses 31-33

Your perception is your reality. The Israelites focused on their fear instead of their promise. And the ones reporting didn't want to be alone in that fear so they spread a bad report throughout the community. As we explored in chapter 1, if someone or something can control your mind, they can control you. They had to spread the fear to counteract the confidence that Caleb was trying to spread. It was easier to forget who they were and whose they were than it was to face the fear and believe that what was promised was theirs. The enemy very craftily worked his way into their minds and they fell for the false belief that they were tiny and worthless in comparison to the people that possessed their land. It was a direct result of that belief of self that caused them to declare, "and we looked the same to them." Who told them they looked like grasshoppers? Their perception became their reality.

Who told you that you were worthless? Who told you that you would not amount to anything? Who told you that you couldn't do something? Who told you that you were second rate? Who told you that you were ugly? These things get hammered into our mind, become our perception, and then become our reality. The result is a broken, hurting person who just wants someone to suffer with them or at least acknowledge their suffering. That is exactly what happened with the girl in this chapter. Somewhere along the way she was hurt, became like a grasshopper in her own eyes and decided to perpetuate that hurt onto others. How you treat other people is a direct reflection of how you feel about yourself. Does that make her actions ok? Absolutely not! Understanding the root of why people act the way they do can be helpful but it never ever excuses the sin.

So who are you? Is the definition you hold of yourself accurate or based on pain and circumstances beyond your control? Are you a grasshopper in your own eyes and as a result truly believe that others view you in that same way? Been there, done that. The good news is you do not have to stay there. What your pain has instilled in you is not truth. Truth is you are valuable; you have things to offer this world that no one else has. You can do things that not one other person on this planet can do just like you. The Bible says we are to renew our mind. Start that process now. The enemy has been in control of your mind for far too long. Let's take a few moments and explore just a little of how God sees you.

Isaiah 43:1-3(a), 4(a)

"But now, this is what the Lord says – He who created you, O Jacob, He who

formed you, O Israel: Fear not for I have redeemed you; **I have summoned you by name; you are mine.** When you pass through the waters, I will be with you; and when you pass through the rivers, they will not sweep over you. When you walk through the fire, you will not be burned; the flames will not set you ablaze. For I am the Lord, your God, the Holy One of Israel, your Savior." Just the beginning of verse 4; "Since you are **precious and honored** in my sight, and because I love you.

Zephaniah 3:17 "The Lord your God is with you, He is mighty to save. He will take **great delight in you**, He will quiet you with His love, He will rejoice over you with singing".

2 Samuel 22:17-20 also found in Psalm 18:16-19.

"He reached down from on high and took hold of me; He drew me out of deep waters. He rescued me from my powerful enemy, from my foes, who were too strong for me. They confronted me in the day of my disaster, but the Lord was my support. He brought me out into a spacious place; He rescued me **because He delighted in me.**"

Matthew 10: 30-31 "And even the very hairs of your head are all numbered. So don't be afraid: **you are worth more** than many sparrows."

God delights in you! The Webster's Dictionary defines the word delight as a strong feeling of happiness. Great pleasure or satisfaction. Something that makes you very happy; something that gives you great pleasure or satisfaction.

The passages you just read say that God delights in you. Think about that. Your Creator not only calls you by name but more than that He delights in you! He finds great pleasure and satisfaction when He looks at you. I am positive it breaks His heart when what the world reports becomes more a part of who we are than what He reports.

- The world says you're worthless, God says you're worth it.
- The world says you will never amount to anything, God says you are already something.
- The world says you can't! God says you can!
- The world says you are second rate, God says you are number one.
- The world says you are ugly, God says you are beautiful.
- The world says you have no value, God says you are valuable.

3. Broken Things & Breaks

One thing I enjoyed doing as a child was riding my bike. We used to ride all over town. Dad was a stickler for rules and taught us every traffic rule you can think of before he would let us venture out on our own. He trained us well and, as a result, we were very cautious and safe while riding bikes. Somewhere in my fifth-grade year, I had gotten a fairly new bike and went on a bike ride with one of my brothers. We were heading down a very familiar hill and he encouraged me to peddle to see how fast we could get going. Although coasting down this hill was fast enough, not wanting to disappoint him, I peddled. Suddenly, because of the speed, my bike began shaking and I lost control just in time to hit a guard rail and slide on gravel on my face. My brother jumped off his bike to help me. My mouth was full of blood, and I had cuts all over me. We walked the almost 3 blocks to home, my brother cried most the way and I just walked. I had hit so hard I was numb. As we entered the house, I quietly walked to the bathroom while my brother explained to Mom what had happened. Mom ran quickly into the bathroom to do what good moms do. As she rinsed my mouth out and began checking, she realized I was missing my front tooth, my already permanent front tooth. She cleaned me up best she could, gave me a cold cloth to hold on my mouth, loaded me in the car and went to the accident sight where somehow she instantly found my tooth. We headed for the dentist. The rest of day was a blur of surgeries on my mouth and a trip to the ER to make sure nothing was broken. The injuries were severe enough that the ER clarified with my mother that I was actually on a bicycle not a motorcycle. The dentist was able to re-insert my actual tooth but gave strict instructions to assure proper healing. For the next few weeks, I had to eat smashed food or milkshakes, and stay off of my bike.

Thankfully my fifth-grade year of school, I had a patient teacher. As the school year progressed, I snapped my wrist and was eight weeks in a cast. I had only had the cast off about two weeks and snapped my wrist again. When I walked through the door with another cast, she shook her head and decided she was going to teach me to write with my left hand. It was sloppy but she succeeded. I can still write with my left hand although never as neatly as my right.

In the midst of all of this, a new Pastor had moved into town. He was young, had a beautiful wife and a baby. He walked door to door in the town meeting families and inviting them to church. I will never forget the day he knocked on our door. It started a friendship that is dear to my heart to this day. He spoke with us for a while and invited my brother and me to come to his home for a youth kick-off party. We eagerly accepted the invitation. For the next several years, we attended the youth group at the church right across the street. There was a good balance of work, fun, and devotions at every meeting. Our involvement in the church became pretty regular at this point. Growing up it was sporadic. We would go for a while then not; off and on for years between that church and another one outside of town. Through the years, Dad served on the church board and Mom taught Sunday school but we were never really permanent church attendees. So the consistency of the youth group and my brother and I going, whether or not the rest of the family did, was new. I became very close to the Pastor's wife and spent a lot of time in their home. She was the first person in my life to notice that something was not quite right. As she got to know me more, she would delicately address things but I of course remained completely silent about the sexual abuse that was taking place. When my home would get out of control, I would go to their home. One day after a huge argument with Dad, I practically ran to their home. She asked what had happened, held me as I cried, and then we went for a walk around the block. While we were walking, my father rode up on his bike and said very sternly that I needed to go home right this instant. The Pastor's wife tucked me behind her, looked my father in the eyes, and said, "She will be home in a few hours, that will give you time to calm down." I was floored and scared to death, but she just stood there staring at him. He eventually turned his bike around and left. At that point in my life I had never had anyone notice my pain, let alone stand up for me. That relationship continued and their home became a very safe place for me. I knew every ounce of that home very well, all the exits, all the windows, everything.

The summer of my sixth-grade year, the youth group went on a mission trip to Kentucky. My brother and I worked hard and raised our money. The Pastor, four youth and one other chaperone headed out. We were going to work for a week at a mission helping to rebuild homes in the area and fix and clean things at the mission. I was excited for the new adventure. That year had also brought an end to the sexual abuse. The group had disbanded, some moved away, others just stopped, and the individuals all stopped after learning that my monthly cycle had begun. The trip was a clean start. I was quite clumsy as a child and protecting me from getting hurt had become a joke in the youth group. Before we pulled out of the driveway, the

Pastor's wife instructed everyone to watch me, especially if we were on any mountain sides. We all laughed, prayed together, and headed out. We arrived several hours later, got settled, attended our first meetings that contained instructions and group assignments, met that night for worship time and devotion, then on Monday began working. During the first part of the week I went with a group to help clean a school that the children on the mission attended, worked on a house, and helped clear a brush field. The day of the clearing, we loaded brush on these big dump trucks. At lunch time, we all hopped in the back and our leaders drove us to camp to eat. As we were getting off of the truck, my foot got caught on something and I fell face first off of the back of the dump truck. As you would expect, I hit a rock and loosened the tooth that had been surgically replaced. Pastor took me to the local dentist but in that area, of course, they did not have equipment like was needed for my situation. He called his wife so she could talk with my parents. Knowing it was not the day he said we would call home, the Pastor's wife answered with "Hello, what happened to Jean?" After receiving medical attention, it was decided that I could stay the rest of the week but I was not allowed to do much. The next few days found me sitting in the cafeteria with the older ladies counting soup labels.

The trip had come to an end and upon arriving home; I, of course, had to have dental work done. It was a miracle that the dentist was able to save the tooth the first time around. The impact of the fall proved fatal for my little tooth. It was replaced with a false one that was cemented to the good one and filed smooth rendering my front teeth pretty much useless. Despite that mishap, the summer was a much-needed break from everything. It was a reprieve. Although damage had been done, it was nice to not be being abused on an almost daily basis. Life went on, but not as usual and I had to figure out a new normal because my normal had changed. I continued to get more involved in church. I joined the choir and the bell choir, helped out with Vacation Bible School, participated in all the youth activities and became closer and closer to the Pastor and his wife.

Middle School brought even more involvement as I joined the band and played volleyball. I was extremely quiet, reserved, and very respectful of others. That was instilled in us by grandparents and parents. Many people liked me and I couldn't quite understand why. The thought that most entered my mind was always 'if they knew the real me, they wouldn't like me'. Truth was the real me was sweet, did want to help others and be everyone's friend. I was gentle and kind and as stated before I never wanted anyone to hurt like I had hurt. But I was oh so very broken. My brokenness affected my relationships. I wanted to be close to others but I had to keep the wall up so I wouldn't get hurt again. I was convinced that something was fundamentally wrong with me, that love was conditional and that surely if the "real me" showed, people would scatter. The "real me", in my mind was a horrible, disgusting person; which clashes with the real me I describe above. Who I was, and who I thought I was were complete opposites. The result of that is a people pleasing workaholic that cries themselves to sleep the majority of nights because the torment of who you are and who you think you are is in a constant tug of war, it's exhausting.

Days turned into years and in October of my eighth-grade year the news arrived that the Pastor and his wife were relocating. He was, by far, the best Pastor that church had ever had but he stood up for a child whose family was very influential and on the board, and that board member successfully got them voted out. It was devastating to me and the majority of the church body. Years later, it was revealed that the Pastor was correct in his reporting and the board member was exposed and removed from the board and shortly after stopped attending the church. Nevertheless, the damage had been done at the time and they were leaving. I felt like a part of me was dying. I spent a lot of time at their home crying and helping them pack. They each gave me instruction, assured me that we would stay in touch, loved on me, and tried to prepare me for their departure day. They also prepared me for the new Pastor that was coming in. They found out he had four children and one of them was about my age. They asked me, if for them, I would be sure to welcome the new family as soon as they moved in. I only agreed for them. The day they left was horrible. At their request, I went over to their home early, spent some time with them, said goodbye, and walked to the bus stop with tears streaming down my face. I remember starring out the bus window, crying all the way to school.

Within a few days, the new family had moved in and very reluctantly I went over to greet them. After introductions, I only stayed a few moments because it was much too difficult to see my safe, beloved home being occupied by someone else. I continued going to church but cried most every service for several weeks. To say the transition was difficult is putting it lightly. I felt like a part of me had died. All the security I had come to know for that short time was stripped away. The only people who had noticed my pain, gone. Broken again. One more lock on my heart, one more brick in the wall I hid behind so well.

When we read through the Bible there are many

stories of good people who had undeserved trouble heaped on them over and over and over. Although many come to mind, I would like to focus for a moment on Joseph. In Genesis chapter 37 we learn that Joseph was the youngest of Jacob's or Israel's sons. He was favored by his father and his older brothers resented that. In fact, within a matter of just a few verses we read that they actually hated him and each time he spoke with them their hate for him grew. Now in his younger years Joseph does appear to be somewhat arrogant, so perhaps on some level the brothers had cause to dislike him, but hate is a whole different level. As the years progress there is a shift in Joseph's personality. The arrogance is replaced by an undying devotion to God and a man who portrays integrity. Let's go back to young Joseph; one day Jacob sends Joseph on a mission to go find and check on his brothers and report back to him. As the brothers see the boy approaching they devise a scheme first to kill him but Reuben intervenes on Joseph's behalf and stops that plan and convinces them to throw him in a well instead. It appears that Reuben's plan at this point is to actually protect Joseph and it is unclear where Reuben is when Joseph is sold by his other brothers to the Ishmaelites but it clearly states in verse 29, after the sale, that Reuben returned to the well, saw that Joseph was not there, and tore his clothes. Often in the Old Testament, it references people tearing their clothes as part of the mourning process. Reuben was clearly upset that this transaction had taken place. Upon confronting his brothers about the location of Joseph, he goes right along with them in the deceit of their father. Jacob believes Joseph is dead and is mourning; Joseph has now arrived in Egypt with the Ishmaelites and is sold again. From this point to the end of Genesis we go on a journey through these years of Joseph's life. Used as a slave, falsely accused, thrown into prison, forgotten about. Yet in the midst of his darkness God is preparing him for something great. Joseph remained faithful through the junk. I'm positive he got discouraged. I am positive he wondered what was going on. I am positive he struggled some but he kept his integrity and he kept his relationship with God. In the darkness he was humbled. In the darkness he was molded. In the darkness he learned to be a great leader and in the end he understood. We know he understood because in Genesis chapter 50 verses 19 and 20 while addressing his fearful brothers he says "Don't be afraid. Am I in the place of God? You intended to harm me, but God intended it for good to accomplish what is now being done, the saving of many lives." In this address, not only does he forgive them but he promises to take care of them. Forgiveness at its finest.

Perhaps you read this story and your gut reaction is

"he's nuts!" after all they did to him, if that happened to me, no way I'd forgive them let alone take care of them. Joseph got to a point in his relationship with God where he was able to look beyond the darkness and see the purpose of the darkness. Why some people seem to get dealt more than other people I do not know but what I do know is that when we allow God to intervene, when we allow God to use our story to save many lives, then the devil runs and cowers in fear. I saw a picture that said when a train goes through a tunnel and it gets dark, you don't throw away the ticket and jump off. You sit still and trust the engineer. Why do we put up with so much from people but the second things seem dark and hard and hurtful we get mad at God and we want to jump off the train He is engineering? Learn to see the purpose of the darkness. Is it easy? No; especially not in the moment. And even more especially not when the darkness is brought on to you by someone else. But even then we must ask, is it worth it? Is it really worth it to see the purpose of the darkness? I say absolutely! What satan intends to destroy us with God will redeem if we allow Him to. Joseph allowed Him to, I allowed Him to, now it is your turn. Romans 8:28 "and we *know* that in *all* things God works for the good of those who love Him, who have been called according to His purpose." Trust Him with the all.

4. <u>High School Happenings</u>

Weeks turned into months and the tears ceased as I adjusted to not seeing the same man behind the pulpit. I stayed involved but probably only because I was in regular contact with the former Pastor and his wife and they continued to encourage me to not give up. I, almost out of obligation, (people pleaser alert) did become friends with the new Pastor's son who was close to my age. The following fall arrived and I was now a freshman in High School. Thankfully, because of my older brother, I had several friends that were juniors so I did not get picked on as much as some of the other freshman. Church involvement continued, friendship was built with the Pastor's son and things were beginning to calm down from the upheaval of the year. During conversation one day, the Pastor's son asked me to go out with him. I politely said no and for the next several months he continued to ask. I always said no. Despite the rejections, he continued to hang out with me. A normal afternoon found us working on homework together, except this time, as we finished, he leaned over and tried to kiss me. I pushed him away and, as memories flooded back, I withdrew. He apologized and for the next two months or so we spoke very little. We were still friends and saw each other at church. We just didn't talk or hang out like we had been. The apology, followed by the break from hanging out as often, convinced me he was sincere. One day, he called after school. He was very upset and he asked if I would please come over to his house so we could talk. He said he had just found out something and he needed a friend to talk to, one he knew he could trust. The tug of war between not feeling safe with him and wanting to be a good friend began. I asked if anyone was home. He said yes his parents were, so I went over to help a friend. I stepped into the home, which because of the previous owners I had been in many times. Remember it was a very safe place for me and I knew every inch of it well. As I walked toward the center of the room, I heard the click of the lock. I turned around and asked why he locked the door; his response was because he had to keep it locked when he was home alone. Instantly, I felt myself getting nervous. After all, he had just told me on the phone that his parents were home. He assured me there was nothing to be nervous about and he began talking. The more he talked the more I calmed down. He sat on a chair and I sat on the couch. After a while, my fear became a reality as he moved to the couch and tried to kiss me. I pushed him away as I had done before but the response was not what I received before. A horrible fight began. Knowing the house well, when I managed to get loose, I ran to where I knew I could get out but they had furniture in front of doors and windows that I either could not get to or simply could not get to in time. Last resort was to run upstairs and jump out the window, but I didn't make it. He grabbed my foot causing me to fall and drug me down the steps. After fighting hard, being shoved into walls, tripped while I was running, drug down steps, and laughed at, he got what he wanted all along. When he finished, he thanked me and let me go. Not only was that rape a violation of my body but it was a rape of my safety; a rape of a gift that was given me. The previous Pastor and his wife had made that home a safe haven for me. It was a retreat; a place where I received proper attention, proper love, proper direction, and safety. That day it vanished. The home that had been so special became a place of utter evil. In my mind, I tried so hard to see it as the first and yet the conflicting scene entered my mind; I ultimately saw it as the latter. I ran home, ran straight to my room, and stayed there the rest of the night. When Mom came home, I told her I didn't feel good and I stayed in bed. I had learned over the years how to get it back together and keep going. I don't remember the next day. I don't know if I went to school or not, but I do know I was reminded that I was worthless. I was a horrible individual. After all, I was at his house. This was surely my fault. Just like everything else, this was my fault. I did not want to tell anyone because I had learned to be quiet, and yet I longed for someone to know. I had learned to have no voice. I had learned to keep it all a secret and that is exactly what I did. The months that followed were terrible. The aftermath of that day was almost worse then the attack itself. In addition to the guilt and shame I was carrying around, within a week of the attack things started to unfold. I was sitting in class one day and was called to the office. I went down and was met by the school psychologist. She took me in her office, told me what she had heard and started asking questions. I would not talk to her. I was embarrassed. I was hurt that he was lying but I could not bring myself to speak. He was bragging about what he had done, except of course leaving out the violent parts. Among other things, he started rumors that I was pregnant. The school psychologist told me in order to help she needed to hear my side of the story. I would not budge. I had learned to be quiet, and I was determined to stay that way. After about an hour of attempting to get me to speak, she assured me at that point that she would not call my parents and she allowed me to go back to class. I felt exposed, vulnerable, and hurt all over again. I got home and my mom greeted me at the door with, "I got a phone call from school today." She named the psychologist and started asking me questions. She just told me she wouldn't call; are you kidding me? We did not discuss it much. I never told my parents it was more than just an assault. Mom had seen the bruises on my hip, back and legs and connected them to what I was telling her. Mom told Dad I was assaulted. The next day at school, the psychologist pulled me out of class and while walking down the hallway, she explained that there was someone in her office that she thought could really help me. I stopped walking. After convincing me that it was not a police officer I reluctantly, more out of respect for elders than anything, went to her office. I do not remember who she worked for; whether the police or Children Services, but she had come to discuss the case and present hypnotism as an option. She and the psychologist thought that would help me talk. I refused. First, I was much too logical than to allow someone I had never met to control my mind like that, secondly, I knew if I was hypnotized everything would come out and that was not happening. She came for the next couple of days to try to get me to tell my side of the story. I refused. The only day I spoke was when the school psychologist informed me that it was her job to make sure I had all my options in front of me. This was the day I found out that he had told people I was pregnant. After a few weeks of complete chaos, a letter arrived in the mail from the outside clinician explaining that because of my refusal to talk, they had to file their report based solely on the young man's story and that it appears to have been a "misunderstanding between friends that got out of control". After the arrival of the letter, my father met with the Pastor and they thought it best to agree with the report. My father came home from the meeting and told me that he and Pastor had worked it out and it was finished.

But the rumors continued. His bragging continued. My pain continued. At this point, I somewhat broke my vowel of silence by writing the former Pastor a letter. I did not include every detail, nor did I tell him about all the rumors. I just vaguely described the incident. His response was quick and helpful. He read between the lines and figured out what happened. I was too scared to follow his recommendations because I had already been informed that it was finished by my father. The Pastor kept contacting me about it out of concern and stated that since I had not made the proper phone calls, he was going to. In an effort to put him at ease, I told him it had been investigated. I also shared with him what the letter from the clinician said and convinced him the case was closed. The daily torment continued; I had a lifelong friend approach me at school and tell me that she could no longer be my friend because I was pregnant. I had several baby-sitting jobs around the town and I lost them all except one, because no one wanted someone "like that" watching their kids. I would walk down the sidewalk and feel like people were staring at me. My mom was informed I was pregnant at church. Ladies would approach her and tell her if she needed anything she could call; they knew how difficult it was to have a daughter that would crush your hopes like that, and how hard it was to find out things from others instead of straight from her. Some of my mom's closest friends hurt her deeply during this time with unfounded words because they believed a lie. I remember being at the post office one day and a family I used to baby-sit for was there. The mother gathered her children quickly, told them not to speak to me and left. As I stepped out onto the sidewalk, they were leaving. The littlest girl in the family had her face planted against the back window and was waving at me with tears streaming down her face as the car pulled away. I walked home in tears. The list of hurtful interactions that took place in this time frame is lengthy. I was in the choir at church and the choir always sat up front behind the Pulpit for the entire service. I would sit there and look out and see him staring at me and smiling. He always positioned himself so he was directly out in front of me. One Sunday, it was just too much and I walked out and did not return until that Pastor was replaced.

Mom sat me down one day and explained that with a rumor that widespread and that believed, she wanted me to be prepared that in about six months there would likely be another one that I had had an abortion. I thought, No way! Surely in that amount of time people will see that I am not pregnant and it will blow over. It was a small town; it didn't blow over and she was right. Six months later, it swept through the town that I had an abortion. My lifelong friend mentioned above had not talked to me much since her parents had instructed her not to, however, she approached me at school one day to tell me that at the town meeting the night before it was discussed that I had an abortion and since her mother was on council and her grandmother was employed by the town she was to never speak to me again. They couldn't afford to be seen as condoning what I had done and they certainly did not want their daughter/granddaughter to be seen with such a person.

Falsely accused. Beaten down in ways that I have no words to describe. Horror and torment for months. As an adult, processing through all the junk, at one point my counselor encouraged me to go to the high school and get my records. I called and went and was shocked at what I read. Of course, the psychologist's records were not there but the school records were. I read from teacher after teacher comments like "she is more withdrawn lately", "she seems distracted", "she has been tearful in class", "her work isn't like it used to be", "she fell asleep in class today". Not one teacher ever said a word to me. Not one teacher ever asked how I was doing or if something was going on. Often when we see someone in pain, we do not want the inconvenience of being available for them so it is easier to ignore it. Although disliked by many, I was still liked by some. I felt like I had a dark cloud surrounding me though. One more lock on my heart, one more brick in the wall.

As mentioned before, I lost every babysitting job except one. That family had known me since I was tiny and when asked by other townspeople why they had not fired me, the father said, "I know her and I do not believe she would do something like that. She is good with my children and I will not fire her." It was nice to have someone stand with me again; someone that knew my character and trusted it even though they endured ridicule for standing by my side. I continued babysitting for them throughout my high school years.

Freshman year had finally come to an end. August rolled around and band and volleyball practices both started up again. I remained quiet and shy and was an average student throughout the years. Senior year arrived and plans were made to attend college in the fall. I applied to a few and was accepted by all of them. We visited campuses and filled out paperwork; all those things you do as a senior in High School. Senior nights, senior celebrations, homecoming, senior prom, pictures, etc... Senior year full of hope, excitement, and promise; at least it is supposed to be. I will never forget my eighteenth birthday that year. March of 1992. It was on a Wednesday. Two months and six days before graduation. I was sitting on the couch watching the evening news and they reported an accident that three young men had been in earlier that afternoon. They put the pictures of the deceased teenagers on the screen and, much to my dismay; one of the pictures was one of my closest friends from childhood. In elementary, he was often my "boyfriend". He protected me, played football games to ensure that I was his, all kinds of funny crazy things. We had good talks and lots of laughs. When he was absent from school I was lost. He was by far the best friend I had ever had in those years. We had been friends through thick and thin since the day we met, which I believe was first grade but may have been kindergarten. He had gone to the vocational school our junior and senior years so we had not done as much together as in previous years. Still, it took my breath away. We had a lasting bond that I cannot explain. We never argued, always stuck up for each other, and never missed a beat no matter how long we had been apart. I remember saying to my dad who was watching the news with me, "That's not my Joe, that can't be my Joe." I said it over and over. Not long after the news cast, our phone rang and it was confirmed it was indeed "my Joe". I had seen the picture and heard the name correctly. I was devastated. Happy Birthday to me. Despite the pain or perhaps because of it, I went to Bible Study that evening at a little church that I had started to attend. In many ways I was numb, but the tears would not stop. The next day at school was chaotic. There were counselors all over the place and announcements that if we needed to talk, we could. I remained in my shell and pushed the hurt down.

The week was a blur. The day of the viewing arrived. I volunteered to pick a friend up and she and I went together. The line was long and the sounds were heartbreaking. We finally got to the casket, his mom embraced me and we cried. The hours went by so quickly and yet were so long. That evening at home, I very unwisely decided that I would not attend the funeral the next day. My mom tried to talk me out of it warning that I would regret it but I decided I was not wanted there, that my presence would be a burden, his mom wouldn't notice, people would think I was silly if I showed my pain and I should just go to school. My view of self was tainting the reality of what the best thing was. The result was horrible.

The next day at school all I accomplished was crying and being angry at everyone that was absent because I was closer to him than them and they should be at school. My mom was right and I should have listened to her and gone. It only got worse as the next several days, at school, people would comment on me not being at the funeral and what kind of friend does that. To put the icing on the cake, the friend I had picked up for the visitation came straight to me and said, "His mom asked where you were, I can't believe you didn't come." That is one decision I will always regret.

As it does, time kept moving. When you are hurting to that extreme, you just want everything to stop but it doesn't. Life keeps happening and responsibilities are still present. Memorial Day came and his stone was set. I went to the cemetery and stood there for quite a while; staring at his stone, staring at my birthday being listed as his death day, remembering all the years together and wiping tears as they ran down my face. Suddenly I felt hands on my shoulders. I turned to see his mom. I have visited his grave several times over the years and many of those times in the early years, his mom would show up at about the same time. Sometimes we talked; sometimes we remained silent. Tragedy, grief, disappointment in myself for having a self-centered pity party when I should have been saying goodbye to a dear dear friend. One more lock on my heart, one more brick in the wall.

"For you created my inmost being; you knit me together in my mother's womb. I praise you because I am fearfully and wonderfully made; your works are wonderful, I know that full well. My frame was not hidden from you when I was made in the secret place. When I was woven together in the depths of the earth, your eyes saw my unformed body. All the days ordained for me were written in your book before one of them came to be." Psalm 139:13-16

If He knew my days before one of them came to be, why did He allow me to be born? Have you ever asked yourself that question? "God, if you knew what was going to happen to me, what my life would entail; Why? Why create me just to endure heartache after heartache and loss after loss?" Stick with me here. He knew your days. He had your path laid out. He knew the plans He had for you, and they were good. Then life happened, choices were made, whether by you or someone else, choices were made that derailed that perfect plan. That doesn't mean the plan is gone; that means it was derailed by choices. God always redeems when satan derails. Remember in chapter one when we unpacked the story of Adam and Eve? The same applies here; my rape and all that followed were human choices. The perfect plan was once again destroyed by a human choice, not by a loving God. Rather than picturing God sitting still in the midst of your pain, picture Him with outstretched arms waiting to embrace you. I believe when little ones hurt, He hurts. I think when we cry in anguish, He cries with us. I believe some choices that are made crush His heart. Mark Chapter 9 verses 36-37 "He (Jesus) took a little child and had him stand among them. Taking him in his arms, he said to them, "Whoever welcomes one of these little children in my name welcomes me; and whoever welcomes me does not welcome me but the one who sent me." He goes on to say in verse 42 "And if anyone causes one of these little ones who believe in me to sin, it would be better for him to be thrown into the sea with a large millstone tied around his neck." I ask you to please stop blaming God for a hurt inflicted by a human. He loved us enough that He created us with a choice and unfortunately there are people out there whose choices hurt instead of heal. The only choice God made for you without your input was your gender. Psalm 139 beautifully lays out the fact that God knit you together in your mother's womb. Once you entered the world, you were being affected by human choices.

The accident I cannot explain. I do not know why some people survive accidents that seemingly should have killed them and others die in accidents that seemingly should not have caused much damage. There are so many different schools of thought on this that we could debate it for months and still not have an answer that would help your wounded heart. What I do know and what I stand on is that "The Lord is close to the brokenhearted and saves those who are crushed in spirit." Psalm 34:18

He is our stronghold in times of trouble. Psalm 37:39

He takes hold of our hand and promises to help us. Isaiah 41:13

He bids us to dwell in His shelter and rest in His shadow. Psalm 91

He gives peace like no other. John 14:27

He is our ever present help in trouble. Psalm 46

He is the one we can look to when confusion sets in. Psalm 121

He desires to carry all our worries if we will just lay them down. 1 Peter 5:6-7

His peace is beyond anything that we can comprehend. Philippians 4:7

He heals the broken hearted and binds up their wounds. Psalm 147:3

He calls me by name and walks with me through trials. Isaiah 43

He is my strength, my fortress and my refuge. Psalm 18

He sustains me when nothing else can. Isaiah 46:4

5. <u>College Chaos</u>

The summer between graduation and college went much too fast. I got a job at a bakery and learned that I had to talk to people to make it work. I did not like that, very much out of the comfort zone I had created for myself. Through a series of funny and frustrating events, one day the owner/manager finally pulled me aside and said, "The customers cannot hear you; you have got to speak up for this to work." It was a summer of great lessons but man was it difficult for me. It all worked out and I was employed by that same bakery full or part time for a little over 20 years.

Summer came to an end and it was time to pack up and head off for college. As mentioned before, I had applied at a few places and been accepted. I decided on one and then literally out of the blue, I received a post card from a small college about 300 miles from home. It was very intriguing and before long, we were down there for a weekend visit that consisted of me playing my trumpet and singing for the music department. Long process short, I was accepted and offered a music scholarship. I loved the campus and everything about it and decided for sure that was where I was going.

At some point in the packing process, my father said to me that he did not understand why I was wasting my time; I was too stupid to go to college. Throughout my entire life he had made sure I knew that I was not as smart as my brothers. In some form or another, I heard it over and over. He called me by a boy's name much more often than by my given name, expected me to do and like many of the things the boys liked, and as a result for much of my life, I believed he wanted a fourth boy and not a little girl. Imagine my confusion as I learned from others that he was thrilled to have a girl and had often talked about his hopes for a little girl and the big brothers she would have. I used to get so angry at one of my brothers because he would often refer to me as "daddy's little girl" and would say that daddy's little girl got anything she wanted and could do anything she wanted. There could not have been anything further from the truth. I often had to stay up way past bedtime and do chores while the boys slept. I was continually accused of lying when I was telling the truth. I would get so nervous that I would laugh, it was my defense mechanism, but in Dad's eyes, since I was laughing, I was lying. As every child does, I did my share of things that deserved punishment but the times I deserved it, I do not remember. Learned from them, no doubt, but remember them like I do the others, no. The older boys often say that they had a much different father than us younger two. There was some physical abuse that certainly the older two received more of than me and my other brother. The worst for me was the day my mother and father were fighting and, as I had done many times through the years, I stepped between him and my mother. This time however, I stepped between them just in time to get hit so hard that it dislocated my jaw. I ran out of the house, jumped on my bike, and took off. We were supposed to be leaving for Grandma's shortly but I didn't care. I rode and rode until a car pulled up beside me and I saw that it was my father instructing me to get home so we could leave. At some point, he popped my jaw back in place. For the entire trip to Grandma's, I held an ice pack on my face. Most nights as a child, I would go to sleep listening to Mom and Dad argue. It seemed like it was constant turmoil in our home. The few happy times were overshadowed by the fear that someone was going to "blow up" and ruin the day, and unfortunately, that was most often the case. As a teenager, I would go places and when people would find out whose daughter I was, I would often be offered discounts or receive special treatment. I hated it. In a particular bad stretch at home between Mom and Dad that resulted in me being late to school several days in a row, I had a teacher that quipped one day, "Well, I'm sure you being tardy so much lately is your mother's fault, your father is such a wonderful man." That was the perception in the public eye. I always wanted to invite people to come home with me for just one hour. I just wanted them to see the professional, calm, well-mannered, intelligent man they saw in public was not at all what we saw at home. More locks on my heart and more bricks in the wall.

Despite the difficult parts of our relationship, which were many, my father did have good points and somewhere in there he did love us. He simply did not know how to show it in a healthy way the majority of the time. He was full of anger, bitterness, and hurt. The more I learned as an adult, I have come to realize that he did much better with us than his father did with him and his siblings. His treatment of us was a direct result of his childhood and all the emotional pain he was carrying. So here we are in August, all packed up and ready to go. We had borrowed my grandfather's van so we could pack things for me and also have room for the four of us. My father, mother, brother, and I headed down south. I was still extremely shy, obviously very broken and I am moving 300 miles away from home where I know no one. Brilliant idea. NOT! We arrived and moved everything into my room. We were almost finished when my roommate came busting through the door, almost literally. She started talking, introduced herself, and threw a bag on her bed. We offered to help her empty her car and it was obvious very quickly that she and I were complete opposites. The next day was a day of orientation for students and so my family decided to go sight-seeing while I attended everything I was required to attend. They promised to come back on Sunday and visit a bit before heading home. Besides the introductions and a few head nods here and there, I did not speak to my roommate. We arranged the room but it was definite separation of sides. My roommate was very outgoing so she had made new friends within a matter of minutes of exploring the dorm. I stayed in the room except to go to all the required events and to eat. Sunday arrived and my family returned as promised. A local church had been present the day the freshman moved in and so we went to that church and then out to lunch. Following lunch, we returned to campus to say our goodbyes. I started crying and begged my father to take me back home. He would not. Although very hurt by his refusal that day, I eventually learned that he was very wise in that decision.

For the first two weeks I spoke to no one – literally, no one. Not even my roommate. I was miserable and lonely. I was so scared of being a burden or getting hurt that somewhere in my broken brain I decided that staying that way was better than building friendships. On Saturday following those two weeks, I had received some letters from various people at home and was sitting in my room reading them. One caused me to laugh out loud for a bit. Unknown to me right at that moment, my roommate was walking past our room on her way to speak with the Resident Assistant to request a new roommate. I certainly couldn't blame her for that. Who wants to live with someone that never speaks even when spoken to? My insecurities and intense shyness were selfish and rude in many ways and certainly unfair to her. It was not my intention to snub her, quite the contrary, I wanted to be her friend but, in my mind, I didn't want to be a burden. In my mind, she would be much better off without me. There were times I wanted to answer her and could not bring myself to do so, I was paralyzed in fear and a shame-based view of self and that affected every relationship built for years. Nevertheless, she heard me laughing and stopped. When she came in our room, she had a smile on her face and took the opportunity to ask me if I would help her put our new fan in the window. It was a neat fan; it had double blades, one blew out and one blew in and it cooled the room very effectively. I nodded; we unpacked it, opened the window, and began trying to situate it. Our room was on the top floor of the dorm. No communication resulted in us dropping the fan, watching it hit the ground below, and break into pieces. She looked at me and said, "I bet if we talked this would work better." We looked at each other, looked at the broken fan, and started laughing. We began talking that day and became very good friends over the course of the year. In case you are wondering, we did get the fan fixed and put in the window safely.

Second semester arrived and for some reason my advisor decided I could handle 24 credit hours. I found out a few years later, that was unheard of for a college freshman and should have never happened but, nevertheless, there I was in classes everyday from 7:55am until 9pm. I struggled. I withdrew from others even more. I was miserable. My roommate said she had something that would help with the stress and so began an addiction. The enemy was clever. My particular drug of choice had the opposite effect on me than it had on most people. I was energetic, I was confident, my grades improved, stress reduced, my appetite decreased, and I never had to pay a dime for my supply. I was doing well, so I thought. In reality, I was spiraling out of control. I was so busy, and consistently so high that I forgot to eat. From January to March, I dropped from a size 18 to a size 10. I came home in March for my great-grandmother's funeral and, while shopping for a new dress, was scolded because the only one that fit was an 8-10. No inquires as to why the drop in weight, just anger. I returned to college and kept on the path of destruction. At one point, I learned that one of my abusers was getting married to a lady who had a young girl. I was terrified that the child would be hurt and decided I needed to confront that in an effort to protect the little girl. I was in no condition to do a confrontation. I had done no work on myself at that point and the result was a disastrous and extremely painful discussion that ended with me feeling like I had made up the memory, that all of it was my fault, and that I was horrible to even think he would hurt a child. It confirmed in my broken mind the already present thought that I was disgusting, worthless, and unlovable. One more lock on my heart; one more brick in the wall.

Not long after that horrific phone call, I decided that life was not worth living anymore and I created a plan to end my life. The weekend arrived that I knew my roommate was going home; I was going to wait until Saturday so I knew she wouldn't come back for something. She was very concerned about me and called twice Friday evening. I assured her I was fine. Saturday arrived, the evening came, campus was quiet and I began swallowing aspirin. Taking pills is not my strong suit; I have a lot of trouble swallowing pills, so it takes me much longer than the average person. About aspirin number 8, someone began knocking on my door. I ignored them for a while, but they were persistent. I finally got up and reluctantly answered the door. My neighbor, a girl I knew but never really hung out with, was standing there. She said, "Please come over to my room, I just learned a new song on the guitar and I want to play it for you." I said, "No" politely but she kept bugging me. I was a people pleaser; my energy for arguing was depleted, so I reluctantly went to her room. The song was "Amazing Grace". She kept me in her room for quite a while playing and singing it over and over. I left her room, and although at that point probably not effective, I made myself throw up to try to get some of the aspirin out of my system and went to bed. I continued to struggle. I was extremely depressed and I thought of suicide quite often but never tried to carry it out again that year. I somehow survived the semester and passed every class.

Summer at home was difficult. It took my mom the entire summer to get my stomach to where I could actually eat something. By the time August rolled back around and I was headed to school I could eat half a sandwich and keep it down. The first half of my sophomore year was better. The roommate from my freshman year had decided to move off of campus and so I had to select someone else to live with. The nice thing about being a sophomore is that you get to choose. There was a girl in our choir who could sing like an angel, was absolutely beautiful, funny, and friendly. I had a few other music classes with her as well. I kept looking at her across the room and decided that no one like her would want to be my roommate. Then suddenly, I saw her walking toward me. I was shocked when she asked ME if I would like to be HER roommate. Little did I know what God was up to. She was raised in church, she knew how to pray, and the only music in our room was Christian. She, often on weekends, sometimes a weekday evening, would go somewhere to play and sing for revivals or special services and so as our friendship grew, I began traveling with her. I just tagged along so I could hear her sing but obviously I heard many a sermon and I was exposed to and introduced to things about God that I had never heard or known. I was curious but also knew I was not special enough, that surely this freedom and healing they all talked about was not for someone like me. I was pretty tainted; why would God want me? I had accepted Christ as my Savior at the age of 16 while at a retreat with my mom and my grandma and although He was important to me and things had been instilled as a child, I was so broken that the hopeful part of a relationship with God had long been pressed down. Wanted it? Yes. Believed it was for me? Absolutely not. My roommate and I had many good times together and very quickly became best of friends. We are still best friends to this day. All too soon the semester was over and she was making plans to be married that summer and quit living on campus. The second half of the year found me in a single room and in psychology and sociology classes that were stirring up memories I did not want to have. My roommate from freshman year was also still a close friend and I began hanging out with her more often, but this time she was off campus so we did not have to be as cautious. In addition to being supplied with what got me through the end of my freshman year, I began taking things to help me stay awake because sleep brought nightmares. Again, my appetite left, I did eat some but continued to lose weight. I went to my sociology class one day stoned. I never missed that class. It was a Tuesday Thursday class and my Tuesday Thursday's were packed. Because they were only two days a week, those classes were an hour and a half. His class was the best 3 hours of my week. It was taught by a full-blooded Indian who not only was an outstanding professor but he cared about the students. He noticed people even if they didn't want to be noticed. I was so mixed up; drinking and smoking things I shouldn't one night and attending Fellowship of Christian Athletes the next night. That day in class was different. While dismissing class, he asked me to stay after for a moment. Although I was afraid of being late to my next class, I waited out of respect and fear. Our campus was a "dry" campus. Being caught with or using alcohol or drugs of any kind would get you kicked out of college - no discussion. I was scared that he had noticed and this was my end. The only other time I had talked to him was at the beginning of the semester when I read the syllabus and saw that our grade was class attendance and a huge presentation that would be given in front of not only other college professors but many people from the town the college was in. That terrified me and I decided to drop the class. To drop the class, I had to have his signature. When I approached him, he refused to sign and told me he knew I was only dropping it out of fear and he would not allow fear to squash my potential. I was angry but later learned that he had great wisdom. The room cleared and he asked me to follow him to his office. We talked generally while walking down the hallway. When we reached his office, he instructed me to have a seat, I did. He placed his notes on his desk and then began pointing out Indian artifacts on his wall and telling me all about them. At one point, I politely interrupted and stated that while I was very interested, I did have another class to get to. He assured me it was excused and continued talking. After about an hour of listening to Indian history, he sat down behind his desk, leaned on his desk hands folded, and said, "Now that you are no longer high, I can talk to you." For the next two and a half to three hours he talked to me about surrender and what it really is and entails. He told me things about my childhood and how they were affecting me now, challenged me, corrected me, instilled hope, and prayed with me. The time ended by him giving me a baggie of yellow root and instructions on how to take it to help the persistent cough I had developed from putting unhealthy things in my body. The love of Christ in the flesh. He could have reported me and allowed me to face all the consequences that in many ways I deserved but he didn't. He saw a broken, hurting child and extended grace that I am forever grateful for. Several years later as an adult, I was returning to campus with a group of friends and had planned to thank him personally for not allowing me to drop his class, his intervention that day, and to communicate how thankful I was for him. In preparation for the weekend, I received a magazine from the college that had a beautifully written article about his life and service to the college. He had passed away just one month before homecoming.

By this point, I had become friends with some very Godly people and although I wanted to believe that God loved me, I didn't. I believed I was useless, worthless, that this message was for everyone else, but not me. I began calculating what to do and when to do it. I would hide things from my friends and fake interactions. I carried all of my pain into every relationship and kept people at a distance. I was invisible and I was ok with that, so I thought. Reality is we all want someone to notice, someone to love us. God continued to place people in my path, and I continued to decide it wasn't for me and stayed miserable. Finally, in the spring of my junior year, the pain and confusion were overwhelming. The group of girls I always hung out with were all going to a retreat about 4 hours away from campus. I planned to complete suicide correctly this time, finished assignments, got everything in order, cleaned my room, and purchased what I needed to carry out my plan. I was relieved. That is a tell-tale sign for someone because once a person decides to end their life and they have gotten everything in order, relief comes over them and often, even if only for a few hours, you will see an improvement in their mood. They have an answer to end the stress and pain. The darkness that surrounds someone who has decided that suicide is their answer is indescribable. Often those left talk about how selfish the act was or is. That is accurate, it is selfish but, in the darkness, the only thing the person can see is the pain. At that point, they have completely convinced themselves that their family and friends, the world, will be better off without them.

Friday arrived; the four girls were all excited and

ready to hit the road. I happily helped them pack their vehicles, hugged them, and walked back to my room. I wanted to wait a few hours to be sure they were gone and had contemplated just waiting until Saturday evening so they would find me Sunday. About an hour after I thought they left, there was a knock on my door. Three of them were standing there. They announced that the other one was unable to go and wanted me to take her place. I argued that I could not afford something like that; they said she wants no payment she just wants you to go. I argued that I didn't have money for food; they said they would cover my food. I argued that I had a lot to do; they told me I didn't. They came into my room and began packing my suitcase. I was angry. I found myself in a car heading to a retreat I wanted nothing to do with. The drive was long. Because I was so angry, I didn't speak a word the entire trip there. I did, however, cry most of the way there. We checked into the hotel, went down for the early bird session at which time I plopped down in the seat, crossed my arms, and starred at the floor. The speaker was Jeannette Cliff George. If any of you have seen "The Hiding Place", she played the part of Corrie Ten Boom. The hotel conference room was in three sections and the platform was right in the center. We were to the left of the speaker. She began speaking then after a while stopped mid sentence, stepped out from behind the pulpit, turned to the right and said, "God loves you", turned to the center and said, "God loves you", turned toward our section, teared up, stepped forward and with a loving but firm voice said, "Someone in this section was going to kill themselves tonight, but God wants you to know He loves you. God loves you!" I instantly began crying. She returned to the pulpit, took a deep breath and prayed. Service was over; still in tears I followed my friends from our seats to leave the room. As we passed the speaker, she reached out and grabbed my arm, I can still see the look of love and concern in her eyes. We walked out to the foyer area of the hotel and approached the beautiful fountain that adorned the center. I sat down and began weeping all over again. A friend sat down, wrapped her arms around me and I cried for a solid 2 hours. She never spoke a word; she just held me and loved me. I had never experienced such selflessness from another human being.

Love is patient, Love is kind, It does not envy, it does not boast, it is not proud. It is not rude, it is not self-seeking, it is not easily angered, it keeps no record of wrongs. Love does not delight in evil but rejoices with the truth. It always protects, always trusts, always hopes, always perseveres. Love never fails. (1 Corinthians 13)

That was a turning point for me. Although still pretty depressed I started being involved more in outreach things on campus, attending church regularly, and doing a Bible study with one of the four girls. I got it together pretty well and by my senior year I was a college ambassador and vice president of the Methodist student club. I decided to stay an extra year and add another degree to my already two. My second senior year I was voted dorm chaplain and became a peer counselor. Despite the positions, the struggle continued. To add to the struggle, one of my grandmas died just two weeks after my second senior year started. I will never forget where I was standing at the park when the chaplain walked up to me to tell me the news. It felt like every time I would take a step forward for good, something would happen and I would take ten steps back. I did a masterful job of pushing down my pain while trying to help others through theirs. Not healthy but effective for that season of time.

The chapter is accurately named College Chaos. It was a roller coaster ride of emotions. Trying to figure out who I was, becoming independent, leaving home but being lost in a sea of hurt, struggle, and disappointment. Not long ago, I was sharing with a friend from college that I am completely different now than I was then. The shocked reply was, "I didn't think you could get any better, you are such a sweet person." Truth is, as stated before, I never wanted anyone to hurt like I was hurting so I did everything in my power to be kind although inside I was so very broken. What people didn't know is when I would interact with them, it was then a few days of trying to figure out what they thought of me, if I messed up, if I said something I should not have, if I sounded or looked stupid, what I could have done better or differently. The questions I would put myself through were endless. It was a constant inner war and it was not pleasant in any way. The times in college years that I ran, that I turned away from God, that I pushed Him away are endless. The times He intervened are endless as well. I could write an entire book just on the five college years. Through all of the ups and downs God held me. I often would get very angry with Him because I couldn't understand why He wanted me to be miserable my entire life. Reality is He didn't and He doesn't. Psalm 30 verses 1 through 3 sum it up very well. "I will exalt you, O Lord, for you lifted me out of the depths and did not let my enemies gloat over me. O Lord my God, I called to you for help and you healed me. O Lord, you brought me up from the grave, you spared me from going down into the pit."

6. The Journey

Graduation finally arrived and the journey after college began. I pursued different avenues but eventually ended up back in Ohio working at the bakery and applying for teaching jobs. My first teaching job was at a pre-school. After that year, I switched to Kindergarten at the same school and taught there for two more years. During this time, I became very good friends with another teacher and her husband. I soon found out from them that they were youth Pastors and the church they were serving in was looking for a music director. They asked if I would be interested in applying. I was offered the position and began serving in this church I had never been in prior to the interview. The first year was busy and difficult as I tried to break out of my shell and be a good leader. I helped where I could, I got involved in a few areas other than the music department and I hid my constant fear and pain well. As time progressed, the Pastor gradually assigned more of the service to me each week. He did this so subtly that I didn't even realize it was happening. One week, after doing the Scripture reading and sitting down on the platform for his sermon, it occurred to me that I had done the entire service from start to sermon. He had even asked me to do the ending prayer/alter call when he finished that day. It was after that service that a board member approached me to inquire why I was doing all the work on Sunday mornings when he was the Pastor. It seemed from that service on that things began to go downhill. I kept serving, and as far as I knew only myself, the Pastor and that one board member even realized what was taking place. One week in our planning session, after Wednesday night activities, we went into the conference room to meet. The other person that attended the meetings regularly was unavailable to stay but Pastor said he still wanted to meet and we would fill her in. As the last choir member left, who was also a board member, she looked concerned and asked if we were sure the meeting needed to happen. Completely unaware at this point, I said that Pastor had asked if we could go ahead and meet briefly. She suggested we meet at the parsonage, told me to be careful and left the church. The meeting began, I was on one side of the conference table, he was on the other, the door was open and all lights on. About mid-way through planning Sunday's service he stood up and headed toward me. As he was walking around the table, he made a comment about me being young and beautiful. In many contexts, it would have been a compliment but in this particular context it was out of place and creepy. He sat down beside me to show me something from his tablet. I became extremely uncomfortable with his closeness and physically scooted my chair over. He moved closer at which point I stood up and stated that perhaps we should finish this meeting at the parsonage. He reluctantly gathered his stuff and we walked to his home. As he opened the door and announced to his wife that I was with him, her entire countenance changed. The tension and uneasiness in the room made the meeting seem ten times longer than it actually was. Sunday was finally planned, and I headed for my car.

Needless to say, Sunday was awkward. I attempted to hide it, kept telling myself it was just me, and prayed that God would use me in the service despite the uncomfortableness. I truly wanted to throw up every time I had to sit on the platform with him. I did not understand what was happening until the following Sunday. The Pastor always positioned himself at the door so he could shake hands with everyone as they left. The choir filed out as usual, he shook hands and when I got to him, he grabbed me and hugged me. I quickly noticed the look on his wife's face and felt horrible for her obvious hurt. I entered the choir room to make sure all the robes and choir books were put away. I was asked by the same choir member mentioned above if we could talk after the room cleared. She very sweetly explained why she had suggested the meeting move to the parsonage a few weeks before. This was the Pastor's first church after being disciplined and sent to counseling for cheating on his wife in previous years. His license was still on suspension but he had completed the counseling, so the denomination had reinstated him and assigned him to this church. I was shocked and frustrated. Why in the world would you hire a young single girl and not share that information prior to her coming on staff? From that point on, I made sure that someone was with us or we were at the parsonage for every meeting. I avoided him in the handshake line and the position truly became a job instead of a ministry. I had relocated to that area so I would be closer to the church and things were going very well with my roommate, so I thought. After several months of being scared of my every move at the church, trying desperately to do the right thing and be a good leader despite my pain and confusion, starting a new teaching job, being with my grandma during a brief illness and then her death, I returned home one day to find a letter on my bed asking me to move out. Despite my attempts to talk to my roommate about the letter, no further conversation happened. It was almost as if she intentionally avoided me. In the letter, she had stated that although she understood my grandmother was ill she was tired of constantly cleaning the house with no help. This made no sense to me as I could name several times that I would get home at midnight from the hour drive from grandma's and do the sink full of dishes or start a load of laundry. I vividly remember one night cleaning the entire kitchen, including mopping the floor. I purposely stayed focused on doing my share during that time so the reasoning in the letter was baffling to me. The sudden avoidance of me was also baffling. I was willing to accept responsibility for my mistakes, but I honestly didn't know what the problem was. I knew the cleaning was not the real problem but with her refusal to talk with me from that point on I was left with nothing. In the midst of all of this turmoil, I was invited by a student to attend his baptism. He was very excited and was going to be baptized on a Sunday evening in April. My church did not have Sunday evening service, so it worked out just fine. It was a powerful service and confirmed what I had already been thinking and praying about. I went home and began writing my resignation letter for the church. At the May board meeting I presented it and silenced the room. After some silence and tears from a few board members I was told it would not be accepted to which I replied accepted or not, the last Sunday in May was to be my last Sunday. That Sunday finally rolled around and we happened to have a guest speaker. The church had done a presentation and thanked me for my service prior to the message. When the speaker got up, he talked about how it was obvious that the body was going to miss me but when God tells you to move you must move. He spoke of Aaron's rod budding and faith and then he said, "I will confirm in the Spirit that this young lady is doing exactly as God has instructed her to and I sincerely hope this church will continue to cover her in prayer as she takes her step of faith." I was surprised at how many times I entered his sermon that day. I had never talked to the man. Afterward he shared some things with me that he could have only known from God.

During this time, I had also applied for other teaching jobs. I was offered a job teaching a combined second and third grade classroom at a small but actively growing Christian school. I accepted and was excited and scared all at the same time. At the end of that year the principal, knowing my love was kindergarten, approached me and asked if she should hire a second and third grade teacher or a kindergarten teacher. I excitedly accepted the Kindergarten position and stayed there for the next several years.

During my third school year, the principle asked one day if she could speak with me after school. I entered her office and was handed a letter. As she was handing it to me she apologized for reading it and stated that it was her and her husband's policy that they will not read letters that are not signed, however, she had begun reading this before she realized it wasn't signed. Her husband was the Pastor of the church that the school was located in. She explained at this point that she had given it to her husband and he had instructed her that it had to be presented to me with the apology. She also shared with me that they were uncomfortable with the beginning because it stated that the author had prayed about it before writing. Their philosophy was if you were that sure that it was from God, why not sign it? As I read the words on the page, I could not believe what I was reading. It was a very detailed list of what a fraud I was; that I had an affair with the Pastor of the church and that is why I resigned, that they could not believe that a Christian school would employee me for this long and the conclusion of the several page letter of accusations was that they really wanted their daughter to attend that school in the fall but that would only happen if the school fired me. I was in such shock that I sat in my chair in absolute silence. After several minutes of silence, my boss asked for my response so I briefly shared with her what had taken place leading up to my resignation at the church. I then shared that although the entire letter was false accusations, I would accept whatever she and Pastor had decided in light of the letter. She firmly stated that neither one of them believed a word of it and if it cost them a student, it cost them a student. She then went on to compliment my teaching ability and what a great asset I had been to her staff. We ended our meeting with prayer and a discussion about the pain of false accusations. One more lock on my heart, one more brick in the wall.

      Things continued going well at the school and just when I was beginning to feel a bit of stability return, our principle announced that she was retiring. The transition was beautifully handled, but change is never easy. Under the new leadership, things were different. It was not bad; it was just different. I was personally going through some questioning and some struggling, still never believing that I fit in or belonged anywhere. I did a great job with the students and the families but, unknown to them; I truly believed I was a worthless failure. I had become stuck in this victim mentality and believed that no one would ever understand me and certainly if they knew the "real me" they would not want to be around me. As a result, I was very much a people pleaser. I had no healthy boundaries and the majority of what I did was simply to be accepted, however I also convinced myself that the acceptance was conditional. One slight mistake and whomever would no longer want to be around me. All in my head, my broken messed up brain. As a result of that broken mindset I made a lot of mistakes, I unintentionally hurt a lot of people; I pushed people away and then would wonder where everyone was. I chose to agree to things and then when I failed to meet the expectations I would withdraw. The majority of the time the expectations I had not met were only mine. When you are stuck in a victim mindset you tend to make sure things are presented in a way that makes you appear as the victim whether you really are or not. In many cases I truly was a victim but there were plenty of cases that I manipulated, that I did the wrong thing, that I made an unwise choice and then tried to blame it on someone else. When you are stuck in the victim mentality you are convinced that no matter what takes place it is not really your fault because if they would have just…..(fill in your own blank). The irony of that is feeling like everything and nothing is all your fault. The problem is the battlefield of the mind. I want someone to notice me; I don't want to be noticed. Listen to my side of the story; what do they think of me now? Sure, I will help out with that; why doesn't anyone notice how hard I work? Everything is my fault, oh no, it is not my fault. The list of back and forth confusion could go on and on. It is constant turmoil when a person is stuck in that mental state. When we choose to live there, we are ineffective, unproductive and being controlled by a mindset that is not reality.

Miserable. Some of you reading this are upset because I said, "when we choose to live there". Make no mistake about it, it is a choice. "But you don't know my story; you don't know what they did to me!" It is a choice. Just because you were a victim does not mean that you have to live as a victim. I am not making light of the pain, I understand pain. I am attempting to help you understand that the mentality the pain has created is not where you are supposed to live.

A few more years went by and my love for teaching grew with every new class. The uneasiness of the transition to the new principal had faded and things were running smoothly. A couple years into the new leadership, the staff was presented with an idea that we were going to implement the following school year for a trial run. It was a team-teaching model for every grade. In light of this change, the administration was doing their best to match up teachers that would complement one another. One of my closest friends was our first-grade teacher so I was asked if I would be willing to move up to first grade. I reluctantly and excitedly agreed to the switch. Reluctantly because I loved teaching Kindergarten and really had no desire to teach any other grade. Excitedly because I would be with one of my closest friends who was a seasoned and fantastic first grade teacher; the move would provide a great deal of opportunity for growth. Because of her experience, I planned on taking a back seat in many ways and allowing her to lead the team. I was not concerned about the curriculum because I knew she would be a sounding board for any navigation I may need. We communicated so well when I taught Kindergarten, I had never even looked at the curriculum for first grade. Periodic check-ins to be sure I was keeping the students on track for first grade was just what we did.

In preparation for our new team model, the two of us met together over the summer, went shopping for our classrooms so we would have the same decor, discussed how we were going to run things. With every meeting and every shopping trip, the excitement grew. With just a few weeks to go before school started, I received a phone call asking if I could come to the school for a meeting. I walked into see my co-teacher, her husband and the principle sitting in the office. I was then notified that her husband had been transferred to North Carolina and they would be moving within the next two weeks. Devastation is an understatement. I helped her pack. I even took a couple trips to North Carolina with her and helped her unload in their temporary apartment. I slipped into a depression and the struggle to even get up and go prepare for the school year without her was like carrying a Mac truck full of bricks on my back. I didn't know how to teach first grade. I did not want to teach first grade without her and, to make it worse, the teacher they hired to replace her had never taught before. I instantly became the trainer, leader of the team, and mentor to a first-year teacher. One more lock on my heart; one more brick in the wall.

I made it a point every year before "meet the teacher" night to have all my desks and whatever else may have a student's name on it labeled and ready to go. I wanted my students to walk in and see their name and know that they belong there. Despite the unwillingness to even show up for work, I still made it a point that year. I felt so much like I didn't belong and like I had no idea what I was doing; but I did not want the children to feel that. My room was set and ready to go. Early in the evening, a family walked in and began looking around. I asked them their name. They told me and I watched as the little girl looked everywhere for her name. The name did not sound familiar, so I checked my roster and they were not on it. I showed the parents and talked with them for a bit and told them that perhaps they were in the room next door. The mother became a little upset and insisted that they were supposed to be in my classroom. I finally suggested that they go check in the office and I once again showed them my roster. They left. Although not my fault in the grand scheme of things, I felt horrible as I watched that little girl's face droop as she could not locate her name on any of the desks. Within a few moments, the secretary and the family returned, and the secretary loudly announced that the girl was supposed to be in my room and asked to see my roster. She then apologized that she had left her off of it and told me she would be back with a desk. I was scrambling trying to get everything ready for them that I had ready for the other families. I had put it all away so the room would be neat for the evening. I also had already prepared for the first day of school, which was the next day. With the addition of a student, I had to do one more of everything. The look on the child's face as it sunk in that she had been forgotten broke my heart. I was not at all happy with how that played out. I assured her, that by morning, I would have all of her stuff ready and I was excited she was in my room. The truth was, for the first time ever in my teaching career, I was not excited or even the slight bit happy that she was in my room. I didn't want another student. I didn't want to work harder. I didn't even want to breathe. I resented everyone and everything. I cried as I read through the curriculum. Every time the new teacher would come over to my room, inside I would sink. I just didn't want to pour the little bit of energy I had left into her. I did try desperately to push that down so she wouldn't know. I did help her and I did answer questions. I was kind but there was a battle raging inside. School started and the war inside me continued. I tried not to let the kiddos know; it wasn't their fault I was struggling. Thankfully, because of my switching grades, I had many of the same students and same parents I had the year before for kindergarten, so they already knew me and how I operated. I did well at focusing on the children when they were in the room but, every time they were out of the room for a recess or a special, I would sit at my desk and cry. The papers to grade and send home were piling up and other responsibilities were being pushed aside. There were many other events taking place in my life during this time that were also contributing to my crashing emotional state. Unknown to me, during this time, a few of the parents that knew me well were very concerned and were meeting together each morning, after dropping their children off, and praying together for me. One day, I had walked the children out to the playground and had returned to my desk to cry, which had become a daily pattern. I sat down and within five minutes, my classroom door opened. It was four parents coming to do an intervention. They had spoken with our teacher's aide who was going to keep my class outside until they were finished talking with me. It was a heartfelt lecture in which they voiced their concerns, offered solutions, and help. By the next afternoon, I had a counseling appointment scheduled; Something I never would have done by myself at that point.

I went to the scheduled appointment and did so for the next several weeks. Right about the time I was getting comfortable with her, I went in for my appointment and the counselor said she was going to do the majority of the talking this session. I listened as she informed me that it was to be our last session. No preparation; no clues prior to that session; just finished. She said of all her clients, I was the hardest to tell and she didn't want to hurt me so she just waited. Giving me no preparation hurt worse than if I had known previously. I was in complete shock, felt abandoned, betrayed, and hung out to dry so to speak. It added to my belief that I was worthless and that everyone, who truly knew me, left. I wasn't worth sticking around for. Now that I am in the counseling field, I know that what she did is actually an ethical violation. We are forbidden to abandon clients; however, I did not know that at the time. I was just a job to her and she was leaving it with no notice.

The friend, who set me up with her originally, tried multiple times to talk with me. She apologized and said she had someone else in mind. She had already spoken to them and they were waiting to hear from me. I was determined I was not doing that again. I was not going to let anyone ever hurt me again. I had had enough. I had been through enough. I was finished. One more lock on my heart. Ten more bricks in the wall.

7. <u>Good Grief!</u>

In the midst of everything in the previous chapter, our family had entered a season of great loss. It all began in January of 2001 when we went up for a Super Bowl party at my grandma and grandpa's house; it was the last Sunday in January that year. While there, we discovered that Grandma was not feeling well. Within just a couple hours, we were all sitting at the hospital waiting on results from various tests, not really caring about football. The next month was a lot of time in the hospital; surgeries, blood transfusions, one week in a nursing home then back to the hospital with an infection in the blood stream. I will never forget the day the surgeon came out of the ICU and into the waiting room with tears in his eyes. He told us he was very sorry but he could do nothing but make sure she was comfortable for the next few days. They moved us to a private room and we were there round the clock. She died at 1:30pm on March 5th. If you have ever lost someone close, you know that the next few weeks were just a blur. Funeral preparation, phone calls, meetings with attorneys, helping Grandpa, the list goes on.

Two weeks after her funeral, an uncle died. His funeral was on my birthday. In May, Grandpa had a massive stroke and the other Grandpa had a heart attack. They both survived and after a while, ended up in the same nursing home. On September 2nd of 2002, we lost my dad's father and on December 31st of 2002, we lost my mom's father. From 2002 through July of 2004, I lost a total of eight people, all very close to me; two dear friends and the rest family. Grief was overwhelming is an understatement. I got to a point where I was actually afraid to answer my phone because I just did not want to know that someone else had died or was in the hospital.

It was during all this that the events in the previous chapter were taking place. Although a different type of grief, my friend/teaching partner moving was a loss as well and needed to be grieved. If you have lost a job, moved because of circumstances beyond your control, been through a divorce, lost a pet, had a financial crisis, had anything unexpected or expected take place that involved a massive amount of change, chances are you need to grieve the loss. Loss is not just losing someone to death. Loss encompasses so much more. Sadly, the majority of the world does not take time to grieve; we stuff and run. That is not healthy and often results in someone struggling daily with anxiety or depression. Stuffing is not in God's plan for our lives. He created us with feelings and emotions for a reason. We are brilliantly designed to cry, laugh, rejoice, and be angry, sad, happy, solemn, excited, etc..... I could list every feeling and emotion known to humans but you get the idea.

So how do we cope with such extraordinary pain? I am so glad you asked. The first thing is to simply allow yourself to grieve. If you feel like crying because you walked into your loved one's favorite store, then take a moment. I received a phone call from a parent who had lost a child. They were in a grocery store sobbing uncontrollably and could not figure out why. I asked a series of questions, one of which was, "Are you standing near one of his favorite foods?" "Well..... yes" came the reply. That is a very normal response. Do not shove it down. I completely understand if you do not want to cry at the store in front of others but as soon as you get in the car, let it out before you drive away. Our tears cleanse, our tears heal, and our tears release things that nothing else can release. Please allow yourself to cry; it is essential.

Understanding that grief is a process that not one person goes through the same as another is also essential. People experience many different ranges of grief; it is not something to be afraid of, nor is it something to be ignored. Unfortunately, the world wants us to be "Ok" within a few weeks of a loss, but reality is that is just not possible. The issue is not whether we are still hurting, the issue is it is uncomfortable for those around us and is therefore avoided.

Elizabeth Kubler-Ross was a Swiss psychiatrist who authored a book on death and dying in 1969. At the time, her studies and findings were groundbreaking and allowed a much better understanding of grief and the effects of it. In that book, she unpacks a series of five stages of grief based on her work with terminally ill patients and those who had suffered a loss of a loved one. Before her death in 2004, she had made statements about her recognition that although there certainly appear to be certain things that everyone experiences, grief cannot be encapsulated into stages. Every person on this planet is different and experiences things differently. If you and I are sitting in a room side by side looking out a window and we witness an accident; we are mostly likely going to have the same general report, "the car at the stop sign pulled out right in front of the truck." Although we can agree on the big picture to help the officer out, the tiny details are going to be different simply because of our different perceptions. I will often say to clients, "What did you hear me say?" Not what did I say, but what did you hear? I don't want a parrot; I truly want to know what they heard and how they can apply it to their situation. I recognize that we all see things through different lenses and although we can certainly reach a place of understanding, sometimes we have to be patient and observant enough to recognize that what we said may not be what the other person heard. The same philosophy can be applied to grief. The way we experience grief will not be exactly the same as our spouse or our child or our best friend. It is our grief and must be acknowledged as so. In that acknowledgment, grace abounds for the others around us who are experiencing grief.

A person experiencing grief may be going through some shock and/or denial. Denial is a conscious or unconscious refusal to accept facts, information, reality, or other things relating to the situation they are in. In some cases, shock is what allows us to have the ability to function in the midst of tragic circumstances. You may hear someone say over and over, "I can't believe this!" It is a perfectly natural, normal response. The problem arises when those who are experiencing the shock stay stuck there. It then switches from being a helpful tool to a detrimental lifestyle. Shock creates a sense of numbness but as the numbness wears off, it is accompanied by excruciating pain. Although this seems unbearable at the time, it is important that you allow yourself to experience the pain fully. Hiding from it, running from it or trying to push it down is detrimental to you and your functioning. As the numbness continues to wear off, life feels extremely chaotic and scary. Your brain is switching from the shock stage to the reality stage and that is painful. Do not be afraid of the pain. Embrace it and healing will come.

Probably the most difficult feeling for grieving people is anger. Anger or rage affects many experiencing grief. Anger can manifest in different ways. People dealing with emotional upset can be angry with themselves, and/or with others, especially those close to them. This is a normal phase and is a time to be especially cautious of not bottling up feelings. Anytime anger is bottled, it eventually explodes and when it explodes, it lands on those who are closest to us. If you are not cautious during this time, you could cause permanent damage to a relationship. The anger is important to feel and allow. However, you must put some things in place to help you handle your anger. Talking about it, exercising, deep breathing, prayer, the use of stress balls, journaling, coloring or art of any kind can be a wonderful outlet. Acknowledge the anger, allow it to come out but put some safeguards in place so that damage to others is not added.

Anger's complexity comes because many people are afraid to be angry with the person that died. It really is ok and, properly handled, can be very healing for the survivors. Right before a family member died, she said to her thirteen-year-old daughter, "If I do not make it through

94

this surgery, do not be mad at God." At that time, I had not yet gotten my Master's degree in Mental Health Counseling but had my Bachelor's in Psychology and had been teaching school for a number of years. I remember vividly being infuriated with her for saying that to her daughter. Anger is a natural, normal response. It can be anger at God as you shout your questions and vent your frustrations. It can be anger with the person that died because they left way too soon. It can be anger with yourself for not doing something or being somewhere that you feel like could have made a difference or helped the dying person. It can be just general anger that accompanies the grief. You may hear people say, "I am just angry and I don't know why." Allow them to be. Allow yourself to be. It is ok, and it will pass.

I spoke with someone who was extremely angry at their loved one who had died from a very treatable disease. This person had a good friend who had the exact same disease as their loved one. Their loved one did not follow doctor's orders, did not take the medication properly and, as a result died, for lack of care brought on by their own choices. Their friend, on the other hand, did everything they were told, took all the medications, and are living a happy productive life. Of course, this person has some anger. It is very justified. It is very reasonable. It is very much a part of their grief process. Anger is a great feeling; it is what we do with it that makes the difference.

A natural socially accepted and expected phase of the grieving process is being sad but with sadness comes many layers. Sadness is a sort of acceptance with emotional attachment. In contrast to the shock which is just numbness, sadness is when we are able to start accepting the reality of what has taken place. This comes at different times depending on the situation. If the death is sudden and unexpected it may take a little longer to land on the sadness. Although you may have it with the initial notification we often then flip into the shock and focus on what has to be done and that is when the tears dry up for the time being. It is essential that we do not stay locked in survival mode. Sadness is very important. It is natural to feel sadness, regret, fear, and uncertainty. This simply shows that you have at least begun to accept the reality. It is during this time that you realize the true magnitude of your loss. For many, the loss of a loved one means moving, downsizing, changing routines. The sadness is not just for the loss of the loved one. It is also for all the losses that come with the loss of a loved one. New routines, a new normal has to be established. Life without your loved one is different and can be scary and overwhelming. Often, when we are in the depths of sadness, encouragement from others, although appreciated, is just not helpful. During this time of grief, you may isolate yourself on purpose – just weary of the questions and the energy it takes to be around others. You may take time to reflect on things you did with your loved ones and focus on memories. Often, when we allow the sadness to sweep over us, we just cannot stop crying. We feel empty and sometimes despair. Random things cause the tears to flow. Smelling something that reminds you of the person or finding something that belonged to them. Trying to figure out when to go through their things and what to do with those things. Seeing someone that looks like them or has some of the same mannerisms. Playing their favorite game or participating in an event that you used to always do with them. Holidays, Anniversaries, Birthdays, special family days or events. The list could go on and on. Be gracious with yourself and if you have a friend that is grieving, be gracious with them. Allow the tears to flow. I repeat what I wrote at the beginning of this section; our tears cleanse, our tears heal, and our tears release things that nothing else can release. Please allow yourself to cry, it is essential.

In addition to tears, laughter can be just as healing. If your loved one was funny or you have memories that make you laugh, then laugh. If it is really bothering you, think about why that may be. If it is a memory that causes you to laugh, chances are when it happened you all laughed; so do not shove it down or forbid others from laughing. It is not an insult, it is not disrespectful, and it does not mean you are never going to be sad again; it is simply a fond memory that caused a chuckle. Memories are what keep us going so let them all come. I have witnessed and been a part of laughter that ended with tears as the happy memory also flooded back the pain of the loss. It is ok to have a range of emotions within a few moments when you are grieving. Not only is it ok, it is normal. The amount in which you grieve is in direct proportion to the amount you loved. If you loved deeply, you will grieve deeply.

Another step, some people experience, is bargaining. Often you will hear this when someone is close to death or when a loved one is preparing for a loss of someone dear. The bargaining can be with God, themselves, others, anyone who will listen. It can include questions or statements like these:

"God, why couldn't You just take me?"

"If You let them live, I promise I will stop _____."

"Why me, why us!?"

"I will never drink again if You will just bring him back."

"She is so young, take me instead!"

"I'll do anything You say from this point on if You will just _____"

People facing less serious trauma may bargain or seek to negotiate a compromise. For example, "Can we still be friends?" when facing a break up. Bargaining rarely provides a sustainable solution, especially if it is a matter of life or death. Often people, who bargain when faced with grief, are simply grasping for anything to help ease the pain. "If we could just have her back, we will do better at parenting." "If I could just see him one more time, the pain wouldn't be so great." It is our desperate attempt to just have one more moment, one more conversation, one more hug. If you or someone you know is bargaining, be very careful to not allow it to switch to blaming. We want answers for our great loss so we find someone or something to blame. Blaming turns into anger, anger into bitterness and we have compounded our grief. Caution is your key. If this is part of your grief, allow it to come but do not allow it to consume you.

Acceptance is when we are able to breathe again. It does not necessarily mean instant happiness; it simply means that you have begun to accept and deal with the reality of your situation. Broadly it is an indication of some emotional detachment and objectivity. People, who are dying, can enter this stage a long time before the people they leave behind. My great aunt had been ill for quite some time. She had lost her sister and best friend, my grandma and had faced many of her own health battles. She was hilarious in life and it revealed itself again at death. She had gone downhill enough that the family had been called and told she had just days. She was in her own home, on a hospital bed, in her living room. My mother and I went to visit. We sat down beside her bed and talked just as if she was fully awake. We laughed, we reminisced as we looked around the room. She had the same "love seat" as they called it, that she had since I was a baby. All of the sudden she sat straight up, looked around the room and declared with a smile on her face, "Am I still here?!" She then instantly lay back down and went back to sleep. Those were the last words I ever heard her speak and they still bring laughter to my mother and me. She had totally accepted that her years on this earth were finished and she was delighted at the chance to finally see her Savior face to face. Although we were as prepared as you could be, her funeral still brought tears. We still had to accept her death, at some point,

when it worked into our grieving schedule. Acceptance comes when you realize that you can think about your loved one and not be overwhelmed by pain. Certainly sadness at times, absolutely, but not the gut wrenching, breath taking pain like before. You begin to look forward to things again and anticipate good things to come. You begin to be more functional; your brain will start working again and you will begin seeking realistic solutions to problems or changes posed by life without your loved one. This is the healthiest time to go through items and begin deciding what to give away and what few sentimental things you would like to keep.

If you are a friend or co-worker of someone who is grieving, please keep being just that. Please do not avoid the subject. One of the most hurtful things for people who have experienced a loss is when they return to work/school/etc. and no one asks about their loved one or inquires how they are doing. They do not have a plague; they are just in a season of grief. Keep in mind that about two weeks after the funeral all the cards stop, all the phone calls stop, all the food and the buzz of people stops. Send them a card three weeks out, leave a card or something special like their favorite candy bar on their desk at work. Typically, the third or fourth week after a funeral is the loneliest, quietest time. The world has gone on in its normal rapid pace and the person grieving feels alone and forgotten. The loss of someone dear to our hearts causes our world to crash for a season. We wish, with everything in us, that time would stand still but it doesn't. Be the friend that didn't forget. Be the friend they can laugh or cry with. Be the friend that will listen to their memories. Allow them the space they need to grieve and to get back into their normal routines.

Another thing to keep in mind is, although the funeral is finished, in many situations the work goes on. After my grandfather died and we got through the funeral, I had to meet with the estate lawyer, I had to gather documents, I had to notify all kinds of places, and I had to file certain things certain ways. It was weeks of work in the midst of the grief. Then about the time I was able to come up for a breath, I received his official death certificate. Sometimes, it is hard to grieve when there is so much finality that has to be tended to. Obviously, each situation is different but if you are an executor for someone or if you are the one that is helping in the details of settling everything, it is a lot of work that puts the loss in your face over and over and over again. If a month after a funeral, your friend still seems to be in the coping/shock area, chances are they are trying to get through stuff. Ask how they are. It takes two seconds to send a text that says, "Thinking of you today" "Covered you in prayer this morning" "Love you". Simple acts of kindness can absolutely turn a grieving person's world upside down. That one text, that one card, that one gift card to their favorite restaurant, that one visit, that one phone call, that one smile can communicate that they are not facing their darkest moments alone. Be the light in the midst of their hurt. We often try to complicate things because "I just don't know what to say." Just be you. They need a sincere you, not some fancy group of words. Simplicity that is heartfelt is more touching than elaborate gibberish.

Now that we have taken a moment to see what we can do for one another, let's see what God says about your hurting heart.

John 14:27
"Peace I leave with you; my peace I give you. I do not give to you as the world gives. Do not let your hearts be troubled and do not be afraid."

Joshua 1:5
"No one will be able to stand against you all the days of your life. As I was with Moses, so I will be with you; I will never leave you nor forsake you."

Exodus 33:14
"The Lord replied, "My Presence will go with you, and I will give you rest."

Daniel 10:17-19
"How can I, your servant, talk with you, my Lord? My strength is gone and I can hardly breathe. Again the one who looked like a man touched me and gave me strength. "Do not be afraid, O man highly esteemed," he said. "Peace! Be strong now; be strong" When he spoke to me I

was strengthened and said "speak my Lord, since you have given me strength."

Grief takes our strength and our breath away; God will restore your strength.

Psalm 28:7 (a)
"The Lord is my strength and my shield; my heart trusts in Him, and I am helped."

Psalm 29:11
"The Lord gives strength to His people; the Lord blesses His people with peace."

Psalm 34:18
"The Lord is close to the brokenhearted and
 saves those who are crushed in spirit."

Psalm 46:1
"God is our refuge and strength, an ever-present help in trouble."

Psalm 91:1-2
"He who dwells in the shelter of the Most High will rest in the shadow of the Almighty. I will say of the Lord, "He is my refuge and my fortress, my God, in whom I trust.""

When you are in someone's shadow, you have to be very close to them. When you are hurting, stay close to The Father. He can comfort and strengthen when nothing else and no one else can. Notice also the word rest. When tears are flowing, sorrow is great, work is overwhelming; He bids you to rest in Him. Rest. Rest in His peace, His comfort, His strength. When you can't, He can. When you cannot trace His hand, trust His heart. His strength is made perfect in our weakness. (2 Corinthians 12:9) If He takes time to tell us that His strength is made perfect in weakness then that indicates that we are allowed to be weak. For those of you who think it is a terrible thing to show weakness, tell me please what are you going to do with this scripture and the others like it? Weakness is a sign of strength.

Psalm 91:4
"He will cover you with His feathers, and under His wings you will find refuge; His faithfulness will be your shield and rampart."

Psalm 119:76-77
"May your unfailing love be my comfort, according to your promise to your servant. Let your compassion come to me that I may live, for your law is my delight."

1 Peter 5:7
"Cast all your anxiety on Him because He cares for you."

Matthew 5:4
"Blessed are those who mourn for they shall be comforted."

2 Corinthians 1:3-5
"Praise be to the God and Father of our Lord Jesus Christ, the Father of compassion and the God of all comfort, who comforts us in all our troubles, so that we can comfort those in any trouble with the comfort we ourselves have received from God. For just as the sufferings of Christ flow over into our lives, so also through Christ our comfort overflows."

<u>Isaiah 46:4</u>
"Even to your old age and gray hairs I am He, I am He who will sustain you. I have made you and I will carry you; I will sustain you and I will rescue you."

<u>Isaiah 49:13</u>
"Shout for joy, O heavens; rejoice O earth; burst into song, O mountains! For the Lord comforts His people and will have compassion on His afflicted ones."

<u>Isaiah 51:12(a)</u>
"I, even I am He who comforts you."

<u>Isaiah 66:13(a)</u>
"As a mother comforts her child, so will I comfort you;"

8. Climbing the Mountain

I finally reached a point where I realized my need and decided to call the second counselor my friend had referred me to. I called several times and hung up before finally letting it go to voicemail. Fear was huge. I wasn't sure if I wanted to try again but I knew my life was crumbling and I had no answers. The counselor called me back that afternoon while my students were in a special. We talked briefly and set up our first appointment. As you may imagine, I was terrified to go to that session. Following the first session, which was a lot of assessments and questions, I decided I would not return and yet something told me I needed to. Reluctantly, I made my way week after week. It was a 45-minute drive from school and the trip home was a little over an hour; yet I continued to go. The first several sessions were a wrestling match in my head. I knew I needed to do the work; I wanted to be healed but I was scared to do the hard work required. Going to counseling forces you to step out of your comfort zone; it forces you to step into a realm that will replace your normal with a new normal. I knew I was broken, and it was affecting many areas of my life, but it was my normal and, therefore, very comfortable. I had learned how to cope, survive and keep on going. The problem is, when we are broken, the coping is really just avoiding and the going is not effective, instead it is a chore. Some days, breathing was a chore; let alone doing everything my job and life required of me. As I mentioned in chapter 6, I had no voice when it came to my past and as a result of the first counseling debacle, it was even harder to find that voice. I have no doubt, that the first few sessions with my new counselor were frustrating for her. I often would barely answer her questions and a few sessions I literally just sat and stared at her. She was patient and would often just stop asking questions and ask me if I would like to pray. She then came up with the brilliant idea of having me write and bring it in. I have always enjoyed writing, so that worked wonderfully. For the next several months, I would take my journal in, read it to her, and then we were able to process the events. She told me, at one point, that she supervised my first counselor specifically for my case and she had often wished that she could be my counselor. That was encouraging to me in a unique way. So here we were plowing through the junk, tearing up the soil that I was so rooted in, unlocking all the locks I had placed on my heart, and piece by piece tearing down the wall that I had so effectively built over the years. It was a difficult but necessary process.

During the process, life kept going so new challenges, hurts, and bumps in the road were occurring. Remember in chapter 6, the letter full of false accusations? I said I knew who wrote the letter, and it was confirmed later that I was correct. This was the day it was confirmed. I sat down after school and opened my work e-mail and had received an e-mail from an address I did not recognize. As I opened it, I quickly recognized the name; it was from the very person whom those several years earlier had written that letter. Her e-mail went into detail about the letter she had written and then concluded with a half-baked apology that was in no way sincere, inquiries into whether or not I was still teaching at that school, and what influence I had in decision making for that school. At the end of the e-mail she told me her husband was applying for a position and she was afraid the lies she told would hinder that. I say half-baked apology because the wording lent itself to someone scrambling to clear their name before her husband's interview happened. The fact that it had been six years since the letter was also a confirmation that it was all made up accusations. Guilt has a tendency to weigh us down. I sincerely wanted the apology to be real, but it was not. I printed out the e-mail and took it to my counselor to get another opinion. Her assessment was basically the same as mine. Although still in the beginning process, I then had to make a decision of what to do if her husband did get the position he was applying for. Because of all the accusations, the stuff she had brought to light in her e-mail, and the ramifications of being under her and her husband, I truly had a lot to consider. I did not want to wait to look for my options but rather be prepared in case he did get the desired position.

In the meantime, the principle of the school had spoken with me about helping another school start a full day kindergarten program. In light of everything, I pursued details and spoke with the other school on the phone several times. When I was told that the family mentioned above did in fact receive the position and would be moving back to the area, I set up an interview with the other school. I had decided that serving under them again would not be a good idea. The superintendent told me that the position was mine and communicated their excitement about the building of their Kindergarten classrooms. I resigned my position at the school where I had taught for ten years and while finishing out the school year, I prepared for the new adventure. My principle congratulated me, told me that he had talked with the superintendent of the school I was transitioning to, and he and they were thrilled that I had this opportunity. I was excited about helping to build another full day kindergarten program. Although the initial plan to move on came when I decided I would not work under certain people again, the transition was so easy that I viewed it as God closing one chapter of my life and opening another. I was scared but I was excited. April and May flew by that year. In late June, I called the school to check on a few things and confirm my start date for the following school year. The principle said that the superintendent was out of the state for her father's funeral and would not be returning until August. She hesitated and asked me my name again. I heard her rustling through papers and a faint "oh no" then she said "I am sorry to tell you this but we hired someone else for that position, I am sure I contacted the correct person the superintendent told me to." Shock is an understatement. No permanent job. Past the time that schools typically hire for the following school year and my position had already been filled at the school I was leaving. All my brokenness, feelings of rejection and sadness flooded me once again. I picked up more hours at the bakery I had been part time at and I did various other odd jobs just to try to make ends meet. In the spring, I was able to get on with a test center and grade school state tests but that, of course, was a temporary job. It was a difficult year and certainly a year of transition and growth.

Counseling had reached a point where we were

doing some much-needed information gathering and confrontations. A family member willingly joined me for a session that confirmed many things I had already processed through and revealed new things. It was during this time that I did the confrontation mentioned in chapter 2 as well as some others. Some went well, others were hurtful, but all revealed more or confirmed information. I had done a lot of hard work. I had accepted my responsibility for certain things. I had apologized for the things I needed to. I had properly placed the guilt and I was working on the shame nature that so affected every area of my life. As we were processing through what to do for the next school year, I had shared with my counselor that growing up I had always wanted to be a teacher and a counselor. It again went back to the notion that I never wanted anyone to hurt like I had hurt. It also happened that at that particular time many schools were requiring teachers to get their Master's degree in education. My counselor smiled and suggested that perhaps with the year I had of odd jobs and not being in the teaching field currently that it may be a good time to apply for Graduate school. She then said, "I think you would make an outstanding counselor." So the journey began. At her recommendation, I looked into a few schools I probably would not have thought of. The next few months were a whirlwind of applications, interviews, and testing. Not only was I accepted to a Graduate program for that fall, but it was also my counselor's and my first choice. In addition, I was also called randomly and offered a permanent substitute position which turned into a permanent job that I had all the way through Graduate school, even summers. They very willingly and easily worked with my school schedule. Let me give you a timeline of these whirlwind months before graduate school began.

In March of 2010, during a daily prayer time, I felt very impressed to read the book of Joel. As we all do from time to time, I argued for a bit with God and I had a bit of an attitude as I read chapter 1. I distinctly remember, after finishing chapter 1, telling God it was boring to which He responded, "Keep reading." I stopped and took a moment to reflect. After apologizing for my attitude, I started over. When God asks us to do something that seemingly to us doesn't fit, we really should just trust Him. He sees the big picture. We cannot see it all; we do not know it all but I am thankful for a God who does. So I started over with a much more open spirit. I read through chapter 1 and cruised right into chapter 2. Chapter 2, verse 18, the tears began to flow. I kept reading and the more I read the harder it was to see. I finished the entire book and then went back to chapter 2. The verses became very personal and as I read promises spoken to a nation they became my promises. Verse 19 "I am sending you grain, new wine and oil, enough to satisfy you fully; never again will I make you an object of scorn to the nations." Promises of hope and restoration are woven throughout the entire chapter.

The Wonderful Counselor began to do surgery when I arrived at verse 25. "I will repay you for the years the locusts have eaten – the great locust and the young locust, the other locusts and the locust swarm – my great army that I sent among you." I paused as tears rolled and I heard Him softly say, "Name them. Name your great locust, young locust, other locusts, and your swarm – name them." It did not take me long to put people from my life in each category. When I was able to see the page again, I went on and read these beautiful words found in verses 26 and 27.

> You will have plenty to eat, until you are full, and you will praise the name of the Lord your God who has worked wonders for you; never again will my people be shamed. Then you will know that I am in Israel, that I am the Lord your God, and that there is no other; never again will my people be shamed.

To tell a survivor of horrific abuse, of any kind, that never again will they be shamed is huge. It is almost unbelievable to wrap one's brain around the shame-based nature being eliminated.

Let's explore shame a bit. The Webster's Dictionary defines shame as a painful emotion caused by consciousness of guilt, shortcoming or impropriety.

The susceptibility to such emotion. (*Have you no shame?*)

A condition of humiliating disgrace or disrepute. *(The shame of being arrested)*

Something that brings censure or reproach. Something to be regretted. *(Pity, it's a shame you can't go.)*

Shame is basically the recognition of wrongdoing but the inability to properly separate oneself from the wrongful act. We process shame as "I am a failure", "I am a mistake", and "I am defective." Reality is you may have made a mistake; you may have failed at something but that is not what you are. What you are is a human being that can pick themselves up and say, "Ok, I messed up. I am going to face it, acknowledge it, and do what I need to do to make up for my mistake." Often someone, with a history of abuse or trauma of any type, lives in the shame-based nature for so long that they begin truly believing they are defective. The guilt that belongs to their abusers, they take upon themselves. You will hear it in phrases like, "He loves me; it is just because I didn't have dinner ready when he got home." "She is not always like that; I should not have come home late." "Oh, I am sure I did something wrong; that is why he/she is acting that way." "Well, you know, I never do anything right." "What is wrong with me?" The problem with the shame-based nature is that it develops into a victim mentality and for some that is a rut that is not easy to get out of. The victim mentality is a developed personality trait that causes one to become very self-centered. In many cases, it allows for attention and validation as others show their concern for you, but that fades in time because when we are stuck in the victim mentality, people get tired of trying to help someone that does not want to be helped. It also allows you to not take responsibility for things. Those stuck in the victim mentality will often say things like, "Well, I would have done it but I couldn't because Marcy wouldn't take me to the place." They are always casting the irresponsibility on someone else. It allows you to not take risks so that you can protect yourself from any form of rejection or failure and it causes you to feel like you are in the right. When you perceive everything that happens to you as others being wrong and you being right, that can lead to pleasurable feelings as it circles right back around to the unwillingness to take responsibility. Not everyone that has suffered abuse flips into this mentality but many do. When you are stuck in the shame-based victim mentality, you truly believe that everything is about you. The conversation you cannot quite hear, "Yep, they are talking about me." The look someone gives you or the innocent comment they make, your victim mentality takes in and turns it into a mountain. When I was stuck in this state, I had a sincerely Godly man say one day to me at church, in front of his wife, in the hallway with others walking around, "That is a beautiful dress." Perfectly fine compliment given in a safe environment with his wife standing next to him. My victim mentality heard "He wants you." I wrestled with it because logic told me it was a compliment. Victim mentality told me he was just like every other man and he just wanted me for sex. Thankfully, I was quiet enough and I knew logically it was a warped thought, so I just wrestled with it within myself.

Living in the victim mentality is complete daily utter torment. Constantly wondering if the look meant something, why that group of people is talking about me, why no one wants to be around me, what a failure I was at the job today, the list could go on and on. Some people stuck in this are very verbal. I was not. I would literally go home night after night and just cry myself to sleep. I could have parents line up after a day of school and compliment me left and right and I would still go home thinking, "Oh if they really knew me…" torment. Absolute torment. So how do you break free? How do you allow yourself to truly believe the words of Almighty God; "never again will my people be shamed?" You step into the river.

9. <u>Stepping into the River</u>

As I continued processing Joel chapter 2 and allowing God to do His healing, more truths were being revealed daily. Verse 28 was exciting to me. To think that even after the restoration there is more was astounding. "And afterward" became two very powerful words. Verses 28-32 describe the outpouring of God's Spirit on His people. Listen to the words at the end of verse 32 "there will be deliverance, as the Lord has said, among the survivors whom the Lord calls." There will be; not maybe, there will be! He will deliver you. He will. He wants to, He longs to and He is waiting for you to accept it. Determination to be healed will put you on the right track to receive healing.

The deep processing of that chapter lasted about 2 or so months. Even with all of my hard work in counseling and this, I still felt like something was amiss. My best friend called and asked me to join her in prayer for a ladies conference that she had been asked to provide the music for in August, 2010. A few weeks later, I received a flyer in the mail that had the conference dates and pictures of the speakers and musician. I was excited when I saw that, not only was she singing for the entire conference, she was speaking on Thursday evening. I called the registration number and spoke to a lady, explained the situation, and asked that she not tell my friend I was coming. I wanted to surprise her. I spoke to my boss at the bakery and asked if I could have Thursday and Friday off with the promise that I would be back in time to be at work early Saturday, because I knew we had several cakes that weekend. The week finally came; I went to work Wednesday ready to go to Kentucky as soon as my shift was over. 1pm hit and I headed south. Traffic was perfect, I could not have asked for a better day of travel. I stopped at a very nice rest area about an hour from the church to change and freshen up. I arrived at the church and decided to park in the lot beside it until I saw the family arrive. My best friend was already there for a sound check. Upon seeing her husband and children pull in, I drove over and parked beside their vehicle after they went into the church. Not knowing the lay out of the building, I stepped through the door which consequently went directly into the sanctuary, and immediately heard a scream followed by my best friend running up the aisle to embrace me. The surprise was a success. It was, hands down, the best surprise I have ever pulled off. I found out later that her husband did know I was coming, the lady from the church had told him just so someone who knew me would know I was making the trip. He didn't say a word to his wife. He was as happy as I was to pull off the surprise. What I did not know, at that point, was that my life would be radically changed in ways I never believed were possible.

Wednesday service came and went. Thursday, my best friend and I went out to lunch, discussed her message for that evening, prayed together, and just had a wonderful visit. Thursday evening, she spoke on getting out of your pit. Years earlier, she had told me that she believed that when I was healed from some of my hurt she would be present. Given everything God had instilled in me, through counseling and through the revelation in Joel chapter 2, when she told me the title of her message, I was sure it was going to be my landmark moment. It wasn't. When the crowd dispersed, she walked over to me and said, "Well?" (in her sweet southern accent) and I instantly started crying. Although I was staying at her home, we sat in the sanctuary after service for over an hour just talking and trying to process the why. I explained that everything I could think of I had laid down. I was hanging on to my promise of deliverance but was discouraged. What was God doing? Where was He? Was I holding back or messing something up? I could not figure it out. Before we left, the ladies director, whom was scheduled to speak Friday evening, approached me and said, "You need to be here tomorrow evening." I explained to her that I could not, because I would be leaving Friday afternoon to head home because I had to be at work early Saturday morning. She said, "Nope, I am going to believe in Jesus name that your boss will call you and say you can stay. God is not finished with you. I'm telling you, you need to be here tomorrow evening." I was disappointed that my time at the conference and with my friend was over. I had promised my boss I would be back so staying was not an option.

Friday morning came. My friend took her children to school, and then we spent time together. I decided to stretch out the time a bit and leave about 2 as that would put me home about 7:30-8oclock. I had only taken enough clothes for 2 days. I had a dress, a jean skirt and two shirts. I began packing and just felt uneasiness. My friend came in the room I was staying in and said, "I know it does not seem possible, but why don't you call work? I think she is right, you are not supposed to go home today." We prayed for clarification. I pulled up the contact slowly, still hesitating on what to do, nervously pressed the call key, and listened to the long ring. My boss answered the phone with, "Hello, I was just getting ready to call you. If you want to stay all weekend, we will be fine. You don't need to come home for one day of work." I was stunned.

Absolutely stunned. I did not even get to ask! My friend and I excitedly went shopping. She bought me another dress shirt that would go with my jean skirt, we washed my other clothes, and I stayed the rest of the weekend. I was concerned about financially missing a day of work but God wasn't. When I arrived home late Sunday evening, I opened my purse and found folded cash in a pocket; it was twice what I would have made that day at work.

Friday evening, we got to service early so she could go over things and pray with the Praise team. When the lady scheduled to speak walked in and saw me, she started shouting and jumping up and down; lots of hugs all around. Although it was a "women's conference" there were a few men present; the Pastor of the church, the sound man, my friend's husband, and a couple of ushers. Service begins. Done with all the announcements, we begin worship. At that point, I had never heard David Crowder's "How He Loves Us". On the first verse, I kept hearing "He is jealous for Jean." It was so audible that I leaned over to my friend's husband and asked him if he was singing Jean instead of "me". He chuckled, teared up, and said, "I can't sing "me." It won't come out today. He loves you so much, sister." As a teacher, one thing I daily instilled in my children was that God loved them and had a plan for their life. My sincere prayer was if they remembered nothing else from Kindergarten that they would remember that. I told other adults and yet I never believed it for myself. I thought I was unlovable, even by God. I "knew" it did not apply to me.

Worship was awesome but that was only the beginning. The message that evening was titled "Step into the River". The scripture reference was from Ezekiel chapter 47 verses one through twelve. Starting in chapter 40, Ezekiel tells us that in visions God took him to

> "the land of Israel and set me on a very high mountain, on whose south side were some buildings that looked like a city. He took me there, and I saw a man whose appearance was like bronze; he was standing in the gateway with a linen cord and a measuring rod in his hand. The man said to me, 'Son of man, look with your eyes and hear with your ears and pay attention to everything I am going to show you, for that is why you have been brought here. Tell the house of Israel everything you see.'"

The next several chapters are the man guiding Ezekiel around the temple area, in the temple, and then into the river that flows from the temple. In chapter 47, the man guiding Ezekiel takes him back to the entrance of the temple and Ezekiel sees water coming out from under the threshold of the temple. The man takes him out the north gate and around the outside to an outer gate that was facing east. The man then begins walking eastward with the measuring rod in his hand and leads Ezekiel through the water. This is where the message for that evening picked up. At first measurement the water is ankle deep. In ankle deep water, you are in complete control. You feel the water. You know it exists but standing in it is very easy to do. The second measurement takes them into water that is knee deep. In knee deep water, you can feel more of the current. It may even cause you to stumble a little or readjust your balance but you still have control. Knee deep is slightly more vulnerable than ankle deep but still easy to walk out of. The third measurement leads them into water that is up to their waist. In waist deep water, your control is diminishing. You still have some because half of your body is out of the water but it is not as easy to walk out as it was when the water was only knee deep. The fourth and final measurement led them to water that was deep enough to swim in. Ezekiel says it was a river that no one could cross. When you are that deep in the river, you have very little to no control depending on the current. The man guiding Ezekiel asked him to truly see what they were looking at and where they were. After that instruction, they returned to the riverbank for the explanation. The man tells Ezekiel that the river that flows from the temple toward the eastern region empties into the sea and makes the water fresh and that swarms of living creatures will live wherever the river flows. He goes on to say again that where the river flows everything will live. The explanation continues to say that fishermen will cast their nets and the fish will be of many kinds. Fruit trees that grow on the bank will never wither and their fruit will never fail; in fact, it says that they will bear fruit monthly and because of the flow of the river from the sanctuary the fruit will serve for food and their leaves for healing. Everything in these verses is directly affected by the flow of the river. Life comes from the flow of the river. She talked about how we often stand on the shoreline and wonder why everyone else is getting their healing, their blessing, their deliverance, their whatever. The reason they are is because they have chosen to step into the river. While we are messing around standing in ankle deep water in complete control of ourselves, they, the ones who chose to allow the river to sweep over them, are living their abundant life in freedom and healing. They do not worry about how they look or what anyone thinks; they want God and are willing to lay down whatever it takes to touch Him. When she finished her message, I practically ran up to the altar. With a broken and contrite heart, I earnestly and sincerely prayed that God would reveal to me what was holding me back. I then made the statement of determination that I had never made before. I boldly said to God, "I am not leaving here until I have deliverance." After praying for a little bit, my friend's husband, who also is my friend, came and prayed for a while and then I heard his voice say, "Come on." A lady stood in front of me. She placed one hand gently on my stomach and one on my head and began praying. I felt like she was doing surgery; the pain that was being released was almost unbearable. Then she said, "You have some people you are ready to forgive. Unforgiveness is holding you back. Start naming them." I started naming them one by one; the list was long. At one point, I paused and she very softly said, "There are more, keep going." I literally felt like my insides were being ripped out, but oh the release. After a while, I stopped and once again I heard her soft authoritative voice speak direction. She said, "Honey there will be more, you have been hurt severely for years. Those who raped you, beat you, sold you, abused you, every time a name comes to you, you need to release them." I was shocked at her knowledge of my life and I did ask my friends later if they had talked to her about me, they had not. When God sends a messenger, He gives them exactly what they need to help whom He sends them to. From that day to this day whenever someone asks me or I have a chance to speak about it I tell people the two keys to your healing are determination and forgiveness.

Determination as defined by the Webster's Dictionary is the act of deciding definitely and firmly. Firm or fixed intention to achieve a desired end. In reference to law it is a judicial decision settling and ending a controversy. Determination is what will keep you going on the days when you feel like going on is not worth it. Determination will define and direct the steps you take toward the new you. Determination is crucial and I will be bold enough to say a different life, a healed life, a free life is not possible without it. You must possess a firm and fixed intention to get your controversy settled.

Forgive is to cease to feel resentment against an offender. Pardon. To give up resentment of or claim to requital. Requital is something given in return, compensation or retaliation. When you choose to forgive you are giving up the resentment that you have held in your heart that has kept you bound for years. You are not excusing their behavior. You are not letting them off the hook. You are not displaying weakness. In contrast, only the strongest most determined people on this planet can truly forgive. It shows great strength and it sets you free. Remember the discussion with the professor in chapter 5? Just like surrender, forgiveness is also a process. Lay it down, speak their name, but if you have a sting sometimes in remembering them or the event, don't beat yourself up; just lay it down again. Just like surrender, you eventually will think of them and realize the hurt was nowhere to be found. Keep in mind forgiveness sets you free. They may never ask, they may not care but you can still be free. In contrast, if you choose to live in unforgiveness you are choosing to stay bound. You are choosing to continue in the daily torment of figuring out what you will do if you ever see them again. Before I had forgiven those who hurt me, I was sitting at a stop light and realized the guy walking in the cross walk was one of my abusers. I had not seen him in years. That was the longest traffic light of my life. I seriously considered lifting my foot off the break and putting it on the gas when he got in front of my car. I did lift up on the break a little but quickly reasoned my way back to proper thinking. I would, however, be lying to you if I said I drove away when the light turned green and never thought about it again. The truth is what I thought was if it would have even been possible to speed up enough in that short of a distance to hurt him. I didn't want to kill him, I wanted him to suffer. Even though the comparison didn't match to the pain he caused me, I wanted him to hurt and struggle for a little while. Reality is that would have accomplished nothing but landing me in jail. I would have still been bitter. I would have still been broken. I would have still been angry that he was the one that caused me years of pain. His momentary pain would have brought zero lasting comfort to me. Retaliation will not set you free.

Until the night recorded above, one of the most difficult things in counseling for me to process was Luke chapter 23 verse 34 when hanging on the cross Jesus says, "Father forgive them, for they do not know what they are doing." My argument was that absolutely they knew what they were doing. I cried, I yelled at God and at my counselor because they did know. They had to have known what they were doing when they chose to do things to an innocent little girl. What I realized later is they truly did not know what they were doing. They could not have realized the impact their actions would have as I grew. They could not have realized the warped thought processes their actions would cause. They could not have realized the nightmares, the tears, the agony, the physical pain, the low view of self, the lack of worth, and the torment they would cause me to go through. They could not have realized that I had no idea what true love was because of their choices. They could not have, in those moments, thought through all of those things so they did not know what they were doing. After I spoke their names and forgiveness flowed that is the moment I understood what Jesus meant when He said,

"Father forgive them, for they do not know what they are doing." I began to view them as people not monsters. I began to wonder what life at their homes must have been like. I began to wonder what influences they had that made them think having intercourse with a child was ok. These things do not, hear me, they do NOT excuse their actions, but forgiveness gives you new eyesight. Forgiveness takes away the revenge mind set, forgiveness allows you to breathe, and forgiveness sets you free.

In John chapter 5, Jesus approaches a pool in Jerusalem. This pool was known for its healing waters. From time to time, an angel would come down and stir up the water and the first one to slip into the water after that stirring would be healed. Because of that, many people who were diseased or crippled or had any form of sickness or disability would hang out there waiting for their opportunity to jump in when the waters were stirred. The problem was it was just one person. So those who had mobility issues often could not get to the pool or in the pool in time. So Jesus walks up to this pool and He specifically approaches a man whom the Bible says has been an invalid for thirty eight years. When Jesus learned that the man had been in his present condition for a long time, He asks him, "Do you want to get well?" King James Version says, "Wilt thou be made whole?" I think Jesus specifically asks in this situation because the man has been in his current condition for a long time. It is a way of life. It is his normal. For him to say yes to Jesus requires him to literally pick up his entire life and start over. It may have been more comfortable to stay there; he had learned how to function with his infirmity. Instead he explains to Jesus the only reason why he is still in his condition. The Bible does not say it but I can't help but think that there was an excited yes in there or perhaps the voice inflection that we miss out on was a resounding yes. Nevertheless, he explains why he is not healed and that he has tried. After the man's explanation, that clearly communicates to Jesus that he does want to be healed, Jesus says, "Get up! Pick up your mat and walk." Instantly the man is healed and he picks up his entire life and walks in his new life. The King James says he was immediately made whole. Within a few steps, he is confronted by the Jewish leaders. No celebration; just reprimand because he is carrying his mat on the Sabbath. He shares what happened to him with them and we discover here that he has no idea who healed him. We do know that he goes to the temple because verse 14 tells us that Jesus approached him again at the temple and gave him further instruction. Following that conversation, the man is able to tell others that it was Jesus who made him whole.

Notice his determination. When Jesus instructs him to take up his mat, there is no hesitation. He realizes he is healed and he goes. He did not whine and fuss because of all the years that he sat at the pool with no one to help him. If he harbored unforgiveness for other's actions, he let it all go that day when Jesus said, "Wilt thou be made whole?" He was determined to start a new life and be rid of the infirmity that had plagued him for so many years. I ask you the same question; do you want to get well? Do you want to quit having nightmares? Do you want to quit being tormented with depression, sadness, guilt, anxiety, and shame? Do you want to walk in newness and breathe fresh air? It does not matter how long you have been in your current state. What matters is are you willing to be changed? Are you willing to be made whole? In your brokenness, can you muster up enough strength to say yes? Can you muster up enough strength to find the determination to step into the river? Life comes from the flow of the river. You may still hit some obstacles. The man in the story above did, but he stayed determined. How do I know that? Jesus found him in the temple still walking around and after conversing with him, it says he went and told them who healed him. He could have chosen to return to the old way of life but he didn't. He went to the temple not only because it was the Sabbath, I have a suspicion he was giving thanks from a very grateful heart. He then shared his story and he kept walking. If you will determine in your mind that you are going to be made whole and you will step into the river then the natural next step is allowing God to lavish you with love.

10. <u>Lavished with Love</u>

As I mentioned previously, I knew that I was unlovable. That this Almighty God could love everyone but me; I was much too tarnished for His perfect love. On Saturday morning of the conference, my friend again sang, "Oh, How He Loves Us." I was still basking in the sweet presence of God I had felt the night before. It had not let up; not even a little. I was sitting in the chair listening to her so beautifully sing, "He loves us, oh, how He loves us, oh, how He loves us, oh, how He loves" and something struck me deeply about the never changing, ever faithful love of God. It was like an ocean wave swept over me and brought an understanding of God's love that I had never had before. For the rest of the day, I was like a child on Christmas morning. I kept randomly exclaiming, "He loves me!" I was so excited I could not contain it. The childlikeness and random bursts of that phrase provided for a lot of laughter that day, but the revelation was so deep and so real that there was
nothing else that could be said.

Let's take a little time to define this thing called love. According to the Webster's dictionary love is:

1. A strong affection for another arising out of kinship or personal ties – maternal love for a child.

- Affection based on admiration benevolence or common interests. (Benevolence is a disposition to do good, an act of kindness, a generous gift)
- An assurance of affection "give her my love"

2. Warm attachment, enthusiasm or devotion. "Love of the sea"

3. The object of attachment, devotion or admiration "baseball was his first love"

- Often used as a term of endearment – a beloved person – Darling, babe.
- In British cultures, it is used as an informal term of address.

4. Unselfish, loyal and benevolent concern for the good of another. - The fatherly concern of God for humankind.

- Brotherly concern for others
- A person's adoration of God
- A personification of love – personification is a person who has a lot of a particular quality and who is the perfect example of someone who has that quality. It can also be an imaginary person that represents a thing or idea. The practice of

representing a thing or idea as a person in art, literature, etc.

Let's take a look at the Biblical definition of love:

1 John 4:7-10 "Dear friends let us love one another, for love comes from God. Everyone who loves has been born of God and knows God. Whoever does not love does not know God, because God is love. This is how God showed His love among us: He sent His one and only Son into the world that we might live through Him. This is love: not that we loved God, but that He loved us and sent His Son as an atoning sacrifice for our sins."

Romans 5:5 tells us that God has "poured out His love into our hearts by The Holy Spirit, whom He has given us."

1 Corinthians chapter 13 describes love like this "love is patient, love is kind. It does not envy, it does not boast, it is not proud. It is not rude, it is not self-seeking, it is not easily angered, it keeps no record of wrongs. Love does not delight in evil but rejoices with the truth. It always protects, always trusts, always hopes, always perseveres. Love never fails"

1 John 3:1(a) "How great is the love the Father has lavished on us, that we should be called children of God! And that is what we are!"

John 3:16 "For God so loved the world that He gave His one and only Son that whoever believes in Him shall not perish but have eternal life."

God is love and He is the source of love. He lavishes love on us and calls us His children. God is patient, kind, He has nothing to envy, He does not boast, He is not proud. God is not rude, nor is He self-seeking. God is not easily angered but rather very patient with us. Once we have asked for forgiveness, God keeps no record of wrongs. He never delights in evil but rejoices with the truth. God will always protect you, He is very trustworthy, provides hope, He perseveres through all of our baggage and ultimately God never fails.

God's perfect love casts out all fear and it awakens a response in those who accept it. The difficulty is that, sometimes, life throws curve balls and this perfect love seems beyond reach. We ask honest questions like, "What happens when life breaks me, and tears flow more often than smiles? What happens when pain is the predominant feeling that invades my heart? What happens when a relationship goes bad, grief is overwhelming, stress is debilitating, and confusion floods my mind? What am I to do when loss knocks the wind out of me, abuse of any kind silences me and sadness engulfs me? What about those days when stress un-nerves me and family makes no sense? Life is dark, pain is real, and there are days that, despite the effort, we feel like love is no where to be found. In addition, you may think that, even if you knew where love was, you feel so unlovable you cannot accept it. I think if we are honest, there have been times when all of us have felt at least one of those things. So how do we bask in the love that the Father desires to lavish on us?

I spoke with someone once who was really struggling with the question, "Is God good, is He really Love, and beyond that if He is good then why is there so much evil?" Why would He create precious children knowing they would starve, knowing they would be abused, knowing they would be neglected and beaten? Why!?" Remember in chapter one, when we unpacked the story of Adam and Eve? Let me take a moment to remind you that innocence is destroyed by a human choice, not by a loving God. We are not equipped to understand everything. We certainly cannot comprehend God to His fullness. The Bible says no man will share His glory. If we could understand everything, if we could comprehend all the ways of God, then we would be equal with Him. We are totally incapable of understanding His ways at times; yet in His tender mercy, God lets us ask the same nagging question that Abraham posed: "Will not the judge of all the earth do right?" Maybe we ask it using different words such as, "Can we really be sure that God always has our best interests at heart?' Or maybe, we just say it silently, letting our distancing hearts speak for themselves. If we are willing to stay close enough and watch long enough, we will discover that the answer to the question is emphatically yes. The Judge of all the earth will do right. He is complete perfection. All wise. Only good. Allow me to remind you of the quote from chapter one; "satan has no more effective weapon in his arsenal than to make us question – not so much whether God exists, but whether God is really good. He knows God alone possesses the power and passion for us to be restored after nearly being shredded in life's killing fields. For satan to talk us into distrusting God and distancing ourselves from Him is to keep us broken, ineffective and frankly out of his hair." (Moore, p. 38-39) The enemy does not come to discuss; he comes to destroy.

The conversation continued with the person asking me to explain Psalm 139:13-16.

"For you created my inmost being; you knit me together in my mother's womb. I praise you because I am fearfully and wonderfully made; your works are wonderful, I know that full well. My frame was not hidden from you when I was made in the secret place. When I was woven together in the depths of the earth, your eyes saw my unformed body. All the days ordained for me were written in your book before one of them came to be."

If He knew my days before one of them came to be, why did He allow me to be born? Have you ever asked yourself that question? God, if you knew what was going to happen to me, why? He knew your days. He had your path laid out. He knew the plans He had for you, and they were good. Then life happened, choices were made, whether by you or someone else, choices were made that derailed that perfect plan. It was destroyed by a human choice, not by a loving God. Adam and Eve's garden dwelling was blissful, and then they chose. I believe that He had a plan, that He had a purpose for my life that was pure and satan set out to destroy it. I believe that when people chose to hurt me, Jesus wept. I don't know how many times God tried to stop them. I don't know how many obstacles He placed in their paths that they chose to ignore. I'll say it again, because I want you to get it; my innocence was destroyed by a human choice, not by a loving God. In His healing love, the love He desires to lavish on you, is when He scoops up all the junk the world dished out; all the hurt, all the abuse, all the grief and He wraps it up and turns all things into beautiful good. If you can grasp this, you will have an understanding of Romans 8:28 that transcends every hurt in your life. "And we know that in all things God works for the good of those who love Him, who have been called according to His purpose." All things. Not some, not neatly packaged only Godly things, ALL things.

The person I was speaking with called me two days later. Knowing much of what my life consisted of, with tears streaming, she stated, "If you can go through all of that, and believe that He is good, that gives me hope." Throughout our conversation, it occurred to me that she was in the perfect spot for God to do a mighty work. She was determined, she was questioning, she was clawing her way through the junk, and crying out to the only one that can mend her broken heart.

Your hurt will tell you that you are tainted by all the things that have taken place in life. The enemy will lie to you to try to convince you that you are worthless and unlovable. In those moments, turn to Jesus and hear the truth. The truth is you were created with a purpose. You were formed and knitted in a perfect fashion; after all you were created in His image. You were created with a beautiful destiny; you were created uniquely and perfectly. There is not one other person on this planet that can do things just like you can do them. Maybe similar but not just like you. You are valuable, you are treasured, and you are loved. Satan is a liar and an identity thief. He takes your power, your authority, your calling, your purpose, your lifestyle, your hope, and your eternity. He cleverly tries to convince you that you've done too much or gone too far but Jesus is longing for you to know that no sin is too big for His forgiveness. There are days you feel like the most messed up ugly, worthless rag doll but God says, "Ma'am, I see a princess, Sir, I see a prince, and I adore you."

His love is baffling because we cannot comprehend it, we cannot wrap our minds around it. Quit trying to. Just allow yourself to experience it. If you could fully understand God and explain Him, you would be equal with Him and that is not only impossible; it is foolish. Satan thought he was equal and it got him kicked out of heaven. Do not put that pressure on yourself; quit trying to understand it fully, just allow yourself to accept it. You are loved. You are loved. You are loved. God absolutely adores you. Allow the Father to lavish you with His love.

11. Restoration Power

When I returned home from that weekend, everything shifted. The healing journey continued but now it was more circular in nature. If you can, picture with me a yard roller. The memory would come, I would tell my counselor, we would process, there was often a grief and acceptance period that lasted about two weeks then the healing. Some things I remembered but had not shared with her, came out during this time. It was also during this time that things were revealed that I had not previously remembered. Allow me to pause here to explain a little bit about our brain function. If you have experienced a traumatic event at any time in life, most likely, you will not remember everything all at once nor will the memories necessarily be in order. Our brains were magnificently created to compartmentalize certain things. It helps with survival in the moment and until you allow the healing to come. I always explain to clients who are recalling traumatic events to not get stuck simply because their memories are not in order, it most likely will not be. Our brains are fascinating and complex.

Repeated trauma increases the chance of internalizing a dysfunctional pattern of alarm state in the brain. With repeated trauma, recall becomes blurred, fragmented, or inaccurate because defense mechanisms (disassociation, numbing and denial) prevent remembering. If the trauma, for example, involves parental abuse, the emotional and behavioral states are more intense and children especially will feel completely out of control and act out of control. Basically, if the external world is chaotic, violent, and frightening, the brains of abused and neglected children will develop and organize to prepare for chaos, violence, and fear. This can also be manifested in adults or carryover into adulthood; often times with adults it will be accompanied with an addiction. One of the most frustrating things in the mental health arena today is the continual diagnoses of ADD or ADHD in children. A child who is suffering any type of abuse or a significant disruption in routine will either act out or withdraw and are not able to focus. It is a very normal response to the present abnormality in their world. Predominantly health professionals slap a label on them to satisfy the teachers and the parents instead of investigating the root of the behavior. It is much easier to label than it is to dig.

In our brains, among many other working parts, we have three basic states: Executive, Emotional, and Survival. The Survival state is located in the brain stem, base of your head/skull area; it is here that we answer the question, "Am

I safe?" Moving up the brain, the Emotional state is in the Limbic system. It is here that we answer the question, "Am I loved?" Up further and to the front is the Executive state, located in the prefrontal lobes, and this is where we can reason and answer questions such as, "What can I learn from this?" "Where do I go from here?" "What is the best way to handle this situation?" If someone is living in a continual trauma situation, they are stuck in the Survival state. They are simply trying to figure out how to live through the next time whatever is happening happens. It is extremely difficult to get someone to reason when they are just trying to survive. The best way to accomplish that is to establish safety and security first. If an individual feels safe, they can begin to progress to the Executive state where talking, processing, and healing can occur.

During this season of restoration, things began to change dramatically. I used to hate spring. Most people love it because of the newness of life springing forth with grass, trees, and flowers; the warmer air beginning to occur more often than the cold, and the relaxing smell of the fresh rain. Spring for me was simply a reminder of pain. My birthday is in the spring, my friend died in the spring, my grandma and uncle died in the spring, the rape in High School happened in the spring, school let out in the spring, consequently two of my three suicide attempts were in the spring, I hated the spring. I am the type of person that easily finds something in every season that I really like, except spring. March-June was excruciatingly painful year after year. It was like a seasonal disorder that caused depression but unlike the usual, which is that people become depressed in the winter, my depression symptoms ramped up every spring. I dreaded and hated spring until God revealed, healed, and restored. The season had been one of my "yard roller" experiences but I did not even think about it until one day in a staff meeting, in the spring, while my supervisor and I were discussing a very sad and disturbing case. She paused and looked at me and said, "How are you doing with this occurring in the spring, is it triggering anything?" I could honestly look at her and say no. As I left the office that day to head to the school, I noticed the sunshine and the flowers that were beginning to bloom and the greenness returning to the grass and the fresh smell in the air that spring brings. It was like having a brand-new set of eyes. In the years since, I am excited about the newness of life that spring represents. No more dreading, no more hating, no more wishing it would hurry up and leave; on the contrary, I drink in the beauty, newness, and freshness that God allows us to experience in the special moments only spring can bring forth.

Numerous things changed during this restoration

season, notably were my perspective, my attitude, my view of self, and my communication. It was in this time that I learned to forgive myself. In Chapter 9, we discussed that forgiveness sets you free, it is a choice, it is an action that communicates and displays power, not passivity. There were things I had done or said through the years that were not okay, some were hurtful to others. I had a temper that was irrational. The root of my anger was based in all of my pain but that does not excuse it. I had to come to the realization that what my pain instilled in me was not truth. As mentioned before, I was very quiet but I did explode occasionally, and I would continually find myself catastrophizing (seeing only the worst possible outcome) things or events in my own mind. I rarely voiced them to others but I sure would let my mind go all kinds of places. I also had a very difficult time receiving correction or guidance. I wanted to receive it but it was a struggle. Although I would not outwardly communicate it, I was inwardly rebellious and miserable. If you would have asked me at the time, I would have had no idea that rebellion was what was causing my misery but once I realized it, my responses and misery began to make sense. I would listen, be respectful in the moment, and sometimes I would really try to apply what my authority said but I constantly battled hurt, thinking the statement was a reflection of who I was as a person. Therefore, if someone pointed out an area for improvement, instead of figuring out what I could do to improve, I would listen but then be sad because I *knew* I was the problem. Jumping to conclusions without evidence – "Great, they think I am a failure." "They will not ask me to do that again, they can find someone that will do it right" Thoughts like "Well, if she would have done it of course it would be ok, it's just because I did it." "I'm terrible at everything." "I bet they think I am a horrible person." "They don't like me." Always internalizing and personalizing, it is called emotional reasoning – the assumption that emotions reflect the way things really are. I would blow things way out of proportion in my mind and then I would act on that irrational thought. I consistently interpreted the thoughts and beliefs of others with zero evidence. As a result of that warped thinking and view, although I never wanted anyone to hurt like I had, and I had a very calm and sweet personality, I did hurt people along the way. I made choices that were not wise and caused friction and tension and I needed to accept responsibility for them. Even if it is not your intent to hurt others, if you realize you have, you need to make it right. I needed to fix what I had control of to fix.

At God's direct command, during this time, I returned to a church I had left incorrectly and after a few months of attending was able to speak with the Pastor and ask for his forgiveness. He suffered at the expense of my pain. The circumstances surrounding my departure were many but they were all things that could have been worked out if I had not been interpreting everything through the root of pain, bitterness, and a spirit of rebellion; basically the victim mentality. In the talk, I discovered that rumors had been started and letters had been sent to him on my behalf that I knew nothing about. My heart was broken, hoping with everything in me that he would trust my words when I told him I talked to three people, who they were, and why I talked to them. I thought my conversations were confidential but, in this conversation, I discovered the people I trusted with my pain exploited it to tear him down. I was crushed, but I knew that if he did not want to trust my words in that moment, I would have to be ok with it. He is a man after Gods own heart, He is a leader of leaders, He is an amazing shepherd to the church God has entrusted him with; he is Christ-like and strives to grow in that role daily. Because of these attributes, despite the pain the situation caused him five years before this conversation, he welcomed me back, forgave me, and through the years God has done a magnificent restoration in our relationship that I am and will continue to be eternally grateful for. There is no equivalent to the restoring power of Jesus Christ. You can search all you want; you will not find it anywhere else.

In a previous chapter, we focused on the promise from Joel chapter 2 that "never again will my people be shamed." Now I want to shift the focus to the restoration. In verse 25, the Lord is speaking and He says, "I will repay you for the years the locusts have eaten." In the King James Version, it says, "And I will restore to you the years that the locusts hath eaten." Restoration is defined as renewal, revival or reestablishment. The state or fact of being restored. Reinstatement – like the restoration of peace. Restored such as a bringing back to a former position or condition – a representation or reconstruction of the original form. Restitution – a restoring to an unimpaired or improved condition.

When life has stripped you of everything, when the pain is great, the confusion is endless, the stress is overwhelming, and all seems lost; God, Himself, will step into your desolate situation and restore. Everything the locust in your life have destroyed, God will restore. It is a promise. The only thing that can keep you from the restoring power of Jesus is yourself. If you carefully read through this entire chapter in Joel, you will see that after the restoration there is more. He does not just restore and leave you sitting there. Verse 28 has two very powerful words "and afterward." After what? After the restoration.

After you allow the reconstruction of the original form and after you are submitted to Him and His healing power, then He can mold you and shape you into that unimpaired vessel and in your improved condition, He will pour out His spirit on you. The end of verse 32 says "there will be deliverance, as the Lord has said, among the survivors whom the Lord calls." Will be. Not maybe, not another day, not just for someone else, God says, "There will be." Are you willing to trust His "will be?" Are you willing to step into the deliverance that He has lined up for you? It takes determination and in some cases some really hard work, but it is worth it.

I promise you, you will not regret it. When God says there will be deliverance, you can stand firm on that foundation.

The restoring power of Jesus Christ has completely transformed my life. When I reflect on who I am now and who I was before the restoration, my mind is blown at the vast difference. Who I am now is the beautiful child that God fearfully and wonderfully created in my mother's womb. Not tainted by sin, my own or the sin others placed on me. Because of my work and allowing God to extricate all of the pain that the enemy was using to destroy me, I am truly restored. I have been reconstructed into the original form God had planned. In that process of reconstruction, I have come out in an improved condition. Much like my new view of spring, my entire life has a new view. I have purpose. I know who I am. I know what my calling in life is. I know where I am going and how I am getting there.

This restoration is for you also. He wants to work the same wonders for you but you have to allow Him to. Nowhere in Joel chapter 2 does it say, "I will only restore Jean. Never again will Jean be shamed." No! This promise is for you. There will be deliverance. There will be restoration. You can count on it. I said it before and I'll say it again; there is no equivalent to the restoring power of Jesus Christ. If you will allow the restoration process to begin, you will eventually find yourself at the top of the mountain.

12. <u>At the Top of the Mountain</u>

In the early chapters, it was the building of the wall in my heart. All the locks that were placed on my heart and all the bricks that helped make that wall strong are now non-existent. One by one, I allowed God, through my counselor, to remove every lock and tear down every brick and break every chain that was holding me captive. I love the wording in the King James Version of Isaiah chapter 61, the end of verse one says "to proclaim liberty to the captives, and the opening of the prison to them that are bound." I was bound, locked up tight and surrounded by a brick wall. Oh, I looked good on the outside and I was friendly and sweet to people. I did truly care about people – that was not fake – but on the inside, the pain was overwhelming and the constant fighting in my head was exhausting. It was like everything people saw and complimented me for was who I wanted to be, and really who I was, but I did not know that or believe it. To be bound and then to be free is a feeling that is very difficult to put into words.

Even in the healing and the freedom, there are still bumps in the road, rocks on the climb, and things that distract and hurt. That is life. Although I have continued to walk in my freedom, I have hit some boulders that have knocked the wind out of me and seemingly set me back. None of them ever set me back to where I was before the restoration but nevertheless, they were set backs in relation to where I am now. In February of 2016, I had a pressure in my stomach for a few weeks. It progressively got worse and nothing I did would make it better. I had none of the typical symptoms for appendicitis but based on location it was the only thing I could think of. I had cleaned my parent's house on Saturday and while I was waiting for the kitchen floor to dry, I laid down on the couch and went to sleep. This is so out of character for me that my mother was very concerned. I kept fighting the pressure and just overall not feeling well until Sunday afternoon. After having several people comment on how bad I looked, I gave in about 5:30 that evening and texted my doctor a general question about the pressure in my stomach. He happened to be close to where I was; he walked in the room I was sitting in, sat down beside me, asked me two questions, then told me I needed to go to the hospital immediately and at check in, tell them my doctor wanted a CT scan. I asked if I could wait until after the meeting that was getting ready to start and he emphatically said no. I got up and drove to the hospital, the whole trip trying to tell myself I was ok and did not need to go. I could just go home and rest. I didn't have time for this. I felt bad enough that I did decide to be obedient and just be checked out. That check out landed me 3 days in the hospital and a surgery. They admitted me on Sunday evening. Surgery was scheduled for Monday afternoon. They explained that surgery would be about 30 minutes, maybe less, and that they were doing an appendectomy with a laser so I would have three tiny incisions. As they were unlocking the bed to take me to the operating room, I looked up at the clock and saw that it was a few minutes before 4pm. I remember thinking, "I will be out of surgery by 4:30 – maybe sooner and probably back in my room by 5:30." I woke up in my room as they were locking the bed in place and taking vitals. My sister in law was putting Chap Stick on my lips and gently rubbing my face with a cold cloth. The room was filled with very somber people; a couple had tears cascading quietly down their face. I looked at the clock to see that it was 8:30pm. I very weakly asked what happened and my sister in law sweetly and softly said, "There were some complications, but you're ok." After waking up enough to actually say hello and goodbye to the family and friends that gathered, the room cleared at about 9:30pm. The next thing I remember is Tuesday morning, the surgeon coming in and talking to me. He explained that he had to call in another surgeon during my procedure because I was literally covered with tumors and disease. He said it scared him because he knew it was diseased, but that is not his area and that is why he made the call. Initially thinking it was cancer, he wanted to remove it all right then, however, the surgeon he called in explained that the diseased areas were actually endometriosis and the tumors would have biopsies run as soon as possible. She assured him they would get me in quickly but with what she was seeing I would need a complete abdominal hysterectomy and she was not comfortable doing a surgery that intense without discussing it with me first. He asked me some very serious and direct questions and discussed the treatment plan moving forward. Tuesday was a quiet sober day of reflection. Thankfully, the room I was in was big and bright and as comfortable as a hospital room can be.

Recovery was slower than I wanted and the next few months were non-stop testing and biopsies. I used up all of my paid time off with a half day here and a half day there to get to all these appointments. Finances were stressful and the preparation for a complete hysterectomy and eight weeks off work was mentally daunting. The pressure was not a whole lot better because much of the pressure was the tumors not the appendicitis, so although pain was a little less, it was not significant. The surgeon wanted to do the hysterectomy in April but I practically begged for June so that I could finish out the school year. June would also allow for recovery to be all summer which fit better because school was out, my team was off because we were all counselors in schools, and my private clients had vacations and other reasons to miss sessions during the summer. My surgery was set for June 7th and was to be a total abdominal hysterectomy with bilateral salpingo-oophorectomy. In English, that means they were going to take every single female organ and part in my body. Even after explaining that people would say to me, "Oh no, surely you will have an ovary" or "Oh no - they will leave the cervix." Nope. Everything, absolutely every female part was to be removed. It could not be done laparoscopically because of the extensiveness of the endometriosis and the tumors. Due to other things my surgeon found while running the tests, I shared my story with her. It was not difficult to do because of the emotional healing that had taken place in my life but the conversation in which she said to me, "Sweetie, there are things wrong with you that are a direct result of your abuse. There are some I can fix and will fix with the surgery but there are some that are just permanent damage"; that conversation resulted in reflection, some anger, and sorrow. You see, I had at this point in my journey come to terms with every result the abuse left with me – except the physical. I had never seriously considered that some of my shooting pains in certain areas were a result of that. I had thought it in passing throughout the years but dismissed it as my body just being weird. When something like that is confirmed by a surgeon and discussed with you, it causes reflection. If it didn't that would cause concern. I was angry that I was the one having to go through this. I was angry that the physical pain I'd had for years actually had a reason. I was angry that I was the one who lost my innocence because of someone else's choice. I was angry that my abusers have children and families and now that would never be a reality for me. I was angry that my mountain experience was seemingly coming to a screeching halt that would result in slipping on a few of those rocks and finding myself hurting and struggling again. I was angry that I would have to be off work, but my abusers had good jobs and were doing ok. Ironically – I do not know if that is even true. I do know that the majority of them have children and that one of them is in prison but other than that I do not know much about them at this point in life – but my mind still went there. How is this fair?! Why do they have jobs and families and I am hurting, struggling, and preparing for a life changing surgery when they were the ones that hurt me. Why!? Why!?

In the stillness of reflection comes great revelation. At some point, I realized that this was yet another section of life that the enemy was setting out to destroy. But God. God in His infinite wisdom, mercy, and grace was walking with me through yet another restoration season. Once again, what the enemy meant to destroy me with God would take, reshape, and turn into beautiful good. I, at first, hoped and prayed that God would miraculously heal me. I firmly believe He is a healer – I have witnessed His healing touch on others and myself but, in my spirit, there was a sense that this was a journey I would have to take. One day, in prayer, God confirmed that sense by showing me what would come out of this present darkness. I was not excited, but I was at peace. The peace that completely surpasses our human logic, understanding, and explanation had flooded over me. There were still tears, there were still days of frustration but in the midst of it all there was peace.

This surgery, par for my course, was met with complications. It was supposed to be an hour to an hour and a half and it ended up being over 3 hours. Before she was able to do the hysterectomy, she had to do extensive bowel repair as the disease had wrapped itself around my intestines and caused almost a fusion of some of the organs. We were told before surgery that the room I would be spending the next several days in was on the maternity floor but was private and was set aside for these surgeries. I asked about a different floor but was assured it was on the opposite end of delivery and that she liked to have her people there because she knew the nurses. Because of the complications, they kept me pretty sedated so I was not aware of much until late Wednesday afternoon. My surgery was 7am on Tuesday. I found out that I was a little closer to delivery than it sounded like I would be and that two of my friends had been fairly vocal about that with the surgeon. I will not go into great detail of the care I received but suffice it to say that my experience following the surgery was less than desirable. I am not convinced that the nurses knew this room was set aside for these types of surgeries. Listening to families call others to announce the birth of their precious one, watching new mothers go to the nursery to feed and hold their new bundles of joy, nurse after nurse walking into my room and saying to my parents, "How are the new grandparents today?" and to my brother, "Hello Dad!" One nurse even asked me if I had chosen a name for my baby. In my entire stay, I had one nurse on a night shift read my chart before talking to me. She was amazing; very gentle, sweet, and caring in all of her actions. She shut my door upon hearing someone in the hallway make a phone call to update family on how close the arrival of their baby was. She apologized and gently asked me how I was doing.

162

When I started to talk about the physical discomfort she said, "No Sweetie, how are you doing?" I tried to stay awake so I could have more interactions with her but after a surgery like that sleep is the norm for a while. She was gone at 7am and I was back to nurses asking me about the last time I walked to the nursery or what help I would have at home to care for the baby while recovering. My daily walks around the unit were necessary for recovery but they routed me through the nursery entrance, through the waiting room filled with excited families, baby seats, blankets, and gifts. Past happy dads talking to their dads about the pictures they were sending and the funny look the baby gave them upon hearing their voice. Laughter and excitement filled the halls while grief and darkness filled my heart. Friday finally arrived and I was discharged. My brother had gone to get the car and load all of the luggage and flowers that had arrived through the week. The nursing assistant on duty that day helped me into a wheelchair and then after turning the corner to go to the elevator promptly and firmly ran the wheelchair right into the wall. Shocked, she leaned over to me and declared loudly, "That didn't hurt, you're ok!" It did hurt very badly and the pause allowed the physical pain to once again be met with the emotional pain of hearing yet another baby being born while we waited for the elevator. Tears streaming, I said nothing – I didn't even tell my brother until we were close to home. The entire discharge situation was horrific but matched the stay. He and I were angry, confused, and hurt but finally home for the real healing process to begin. God had told me previously that it would be during this time that I would write this book. In my mind that meant I had eight weeks to write a book. I failed to account for the fact that for the first two weeks of recovery, I was not allowed to lift anything heavier than a fork. For the remaining weeks, I was not able to lift anything heavier than a gallon of milk. In addition, I could not sit on hard chairs for any time at all and I couldn't sit straight up because of the incision which went across my entire stomach. Typing was an extremely difficult task. My pastor tried to set me up with a voice dictation thing that would type for me but after a short while the current software wouldn't work and the subscription for the new software was out of my budget for the summer. About week five, I was able to set up a TV tray and place things in such a way that I could begin typing. The summer was difficult to say the least.

They had cautioned me before surgery that my full recovery would take about a year to a year and a half. I was super active, always had been, so I naturally thought 'Naaaa, it will never take me a year." - I was wrong, it actually took an entire year and three months before I started feeling like myself again and even then, I would still tire much more rapidly than pre-surgery. Life does not pause just because we are hurting and life was certainly happening in the midst of my physical and emotional pain. All I could do was keep plowing. After the work God had done in my life, there was no way I was going to give up on my faith. I would be lying if I said it wasn't tested in those months but once the determination is inside you and you know that you know that you know God is real and God is for you, there is no turning back no matter what the enemy or life throws your way.

In June of 2017, I went in for my year follow up from surgery and a mammogram. The very next day, I received a phone call that I needed to go to the hospital for an ultrasound. From that ultrasound a biopsy was scheduled because the lump in my breast was so deep that the radiologist was unsure of what it was. Meeting with a surgeon, thankfully the same one that did my appendectomy, listening to all the possibilities and treatment plans, and what the steps were moving forward; completely exhausted me. I was discouraged, done, down, and speechless. My pastor called and all he said was, "Sometimes there are just no words." It was then that I allowed the tears to flow. Sometimes you have to be that voice that will give someone permission to be weak for a little while. If you are the one that needs to be weak for a little while know that it is ok. The Bible does not instruct us to carry one another's burdens for no reason. We need each other and sometimes what is needed is permission to drop your sword and cry for just a while. Life happens and life hurts.

I was scheduled to leave on the trip of a lifetime on July 1st. Driving out west for three weeks. We were going to camp to even make the trip doable. With permission from the doctor, we went but the unknown of the weeks prior, the biopsy that was scheduled for the week of our return, and the mental exhaustion left me not wanting to go. My stomach hurt, probably from stress, and I cried every opportunity I had. I did not want the people I was traveling with to see the tears so I tried to make myself be happy, but I know they sensed my unhappiness. For me, this trip of a lifetime was turning out to be dreaded torture. While driving into our first stop, Estes Park Colorado, I was looking out the window at the beauty that was before me and I literally heard a voice say, "You always say no one could talk you out of your relationship with Christ, but could circumstances pull you out?" I instantly knew it was the enemy. I quickly texted my pastor's wife and the confirmation came with her immediate response that said, "I am so glad you knew that was the enemy. I knew it as

166

soon as I read it." She also told me she was praying that the stomachache would leave immediately; it did. I was tired but I did adjust my attitude and soaked in the beauty of God's creation for the remainder of the trip.

Bumps in the road? Yes. Slippery rocks while climbing the mountain? Yes. Storms and avalanches? Yes. Sand pits you didn't know existed until you stepped in them? Yes. However, in the midst of all the potholes, curves, and trials life throws our way there is sunshine, there is a firm rock to hold onto while the avalanche is happening, there is peace in the midst of the storm, and there is sand that gives way to beautiful lakes with majestic mountains in the distance. Do not miss the beauty of life because the pain has clouded your eyesight.

Remember that determination is one of the keys to your healing. Fix your eyes on things above not on earthly things. Fix your eyes on the God who is holding you in the palm of His hand. Fix your eyes on what He has called you to. Fix your eyes on the battle already being won. Fix your eyes on The Author and Finisher of your faith. Fix your eyes on The Word. Fix your eyes on the future He has prepared for you. Sometimes that fixing takes one day and one step at a time but, nevertheless, you have to fix your eyes.

Remember that you are never alone. A dear friend

reminded me once that the 3 Hebrew young men may have stood alone when they refused to bow but they stood together in front of the fiery furnace.

One day driving to the office, I pulled up to a stop sign that I usually turn left from but you can get to the same place either way. While sitting there, I heard God's still small voice gently say, "How about you go straight today, I want to show you something." I went straight on this narrow country road. No cars in sight. As I am approaching the top of a pretty big hill, God said, "Slow down and look to the right." As I looked to the right a beautiful little white church on top of a distant hill came into view. It had a cemetery behind it as many of those older churches do but other than that it was there alone. I have looked at this church many times before, but I have never seen this church like I did today. After a few moments, I continued down the road slowly and as I got to the bottom of the hill and stopped at the stop sign, God said, "Now look; what do you see?" What I saw were a couple of houses across the street, facing the front of the church. I saw one farm property and house to the left of the church and could see the glimpse of a house to the right. On top of the hill, it looked as if it was standing alone but in the valley, at the stop sign, reality was it was surrounded by houses. How often are we in the valley, with people all around us and yet our view is the hill? We feel like we are standing alone. We convince ourselves we are standing alone. That is a lie. You are not alone and please do not feel you have to fight alone. Find a trusted friend or mentor and share your struggle with them. We were not designed to be islands; we need one another.

Remember that The Word of God is sharper than any two-edged sword, it is your guide, your light; it leads you to your counselor, your comfort, your strength. Pick out some victory Scriptures and memorize them. Hiding His Word in your heart will never lead you astray. After you pick them, read them every night before bed. Think about it; if you listen to a song and then you go to bed, when you wake up what is the first thing you think of? So choose to make it The Word of God. Here are a few to help get you started.

Psalm 16:8 "I have set the Lord always before me. Because He is at my right hand, I will not be shaken."

Psalm 18:1-3 "I love you, O Lord, My strength. The Lord is my rock, my fortress and my deliverer: my God is my rock in whom I take refuge. He is my shield and the horn of my salvation, my stronghold. I call to the Lord, who is worthy of praise, and I am saved from my enemies."

Psalm 91:1-2 "He who dwells in the shelter of the Most High shall abide in the shadow of the Almighty. I will say of the Lord, He is my refuge and my fortress, my God in whom I trust."

Psalm 147:3 "He heals the brokenhearted and binds up their wounds"

Psalm 138:7 "Though I walk in the midst of trouble, you preserve my life; you stretch out your hand against the anger of my foes, with your right hand you save me."

Proverbs 18:10 "The name of the Lord is a strong tower; the righteous run to it and are safe."

Matthew 10:30-31 "And even the very hairs of your head are all numbered. So don't be afraid; you are worth more than many sparrows"

1 Corinthians 1:8 "He will keep you strong to the end, so that you will be blameless on the day of our Lord Jesus Christ."

In Matthew 10:28-30, He bids us to rest in Him.

1 Peter chapter 1 – Let your trial bring Him praise.

Psalm 18:16-19, Isaiah 43:1-3, Psalm 121:1-2, 2 Timothy 1:7.

The list is endless – look them up, jot them on sticky notes or note cards, and place them in prominent places so that you can be reminded daily that you are not in this alone.

<u>This is for you!</u>

You have journeyed with me up the mountain and now we sit on the top overlooking the valley below. There are majestic mountains in the distance and Eagles soaring in magnificent splendor. The wind is gently tousling your hair and life is peaceful and purposeful. You hear the all familiar whisper of the Heavenly Father as He beckons you to climb your mountain. My prayer is that because of my story, you now have the courage to climb. Yes, it may hurt; the stripping process is never pleasant, but the healing and the freedom that await you at the top are worth every jagged rock you may encounter. The healing journey is not just for me or a select few, the healing journey is for all who will put on their boots and climb. Are you willing to climb?

Bibliography

Moore, Beth. Get out of that pit. Thomas Nelson, Nashville Tennessee, 2007.

Scripture taken from the HOLY BIBLE, NEW INTERNATIONAL VERSION.

Copyright 1973, 1978, 1984 International Bible Society. Used by permission of Zondervan Bible Publishers.

Scriptures references noted KJV are taken from the King James Version of the Bible.

Webster's Dictionary - Merriam Webster.com

About the Author

Jean Ellen Sullenberger is a Licensed Professional Clinical Counselor, Certified Teacher, Presenter, founder and owner of Adagio Counseling Services, LLC. In addition, she works full time at one of the Nation's largest Children's hospitals as an outpatient counselor in their Eating Disorders Clinic.

She received her Bachelor degree in Psychology and Religion with an emphasis on Education and a minor in music from Union College in Barbourville, Kentucky. Before pursuing her career in Counseling, she taught school for 14 years. She received her Master of Arts in Clinical Mental Health Counseling from Ashland Theological Seminary in Ashland, Ohio.

She has spoken in many settings including churches, schools, shelters, and recovery centers to help educate and support people on topics of Suicide, Self-harm, Grief, Understanding Depression, and Addictions.

She speaks passionately to survivors of abuse and trauma. She gently communicates value and worth, while guiding others to their healing by instilling truth in them. Her commitment and passion are to educate and support others on their journey through life.

Made in the USA
Columbia, SC
12 August 2021